WITHDRAWN

Freud and Dora

Freud and Dora

The Artful Dream

Phillip McCaffrey

Rutgers University Press
New Brunswick, New Jersey

Library of Congress Cataloging in Publication Data

McCaffrey, Phillip, 1945–
   Freud and Dora.

   Bibliography: p.
   Includes index.
   1. Dreams.   2. Freud, Sigmund, 1865–1939.   I. Title.
BF1078.M366   1984   154.6'3   84–1949
ISBN 0–8135–1056–2

Copyright © 1984 by Rutgers, The State University
All rights reserved
Manufactured in the United States of America

For my parents and Lee

Contents

Acknowledgments ix

1. Introduction 1

2. The Art of Dora's Dream 17

3. Freud on Dora's Dream 41

4. The Meaning of Dora's Dream 77

5. The Ideology of Sex 99

6. Implications 119

Notes 141

Bibliography 181

Index 191

Acknowledgments

I would like to take this opportunity to thank those who took an interest in my work, especially in its early stages. Generous support from the Faculty Research Committee of Loyola College gave me the opportunity to conduct a good deal of the research for this study and to complete a substantial part of the writing. Dr. Faith Gilroy read the manuscript and offered timely advice and encouragement; Dr. Hannah Geldrich-Leffman allowed me the benefit of her learning on several specific points. Dr. Joseph Grennen kindly reviewed the work at a crucial stage, with characteristic insight and scholarly precision. My thanks are also due to Tom Scheye and Dave Roswell for their helpful interest and to Paula Scheye for her intelligent enthusiasm. I owe special thanks to Genevieve Rafferty for skillful assistance, good humor, and moral support.

Chapter One

Introduction

Freud's Paradoxical Eminence

The study of dreams, so long a topic of special fascination, has taken two enormous leaps forward in the twentieth century. The first of these was the publication of Freud's monumental *The Interpretation of Dreams* (1900) in which he elevated the entire topic to a new level of significance in the course of laying a foundation for a broad psychoanalytic psychology.[1] No one who took Freud seriously, or who took serious account of him, could doubt that dreaming was a psychological phenomenon well worth disciplined attention. It seems, in retrospect, an instance of remarkable foresight that Freud's publisher postdated the work so that it might bear the first year of the twentieth century rather than the last of the nineteenth. Freud himself regarded his insight into the dream as one of his most significant accomplishments; in his 1931 preface to the third English edition of *The Interpretation of Dreams* he wrote, "This book, with the new contribution to psychology which surprised the world when it was published (1900), remains essentially unaltered. It contains, even according to my present-day judgment, the most valuable of all the discoveries it has been my good fortune to make. Insight such as this falls to one's lot but once in a lifetime."[2] "By general consensus," writes Ernest Jones, Freud's biographer, the book "was Freud's major work, the one by which his name will probably be longest remembered," and he goes on to describe the virtues by which it earned that status: "It is Freud's most original work. The main conclusions in it were entirely novel and unexpected. This applies both to the theme proper, that of dream structure, and to many that appear incidentally. . . . The book is especially comprehensive. (The main topic, the investigation of dream life, was carried out with such detailed thoroughness that the conclusions have experienced only a minimum of modification or addition in the half century since the book was published. Of very few important scientific works can this be said."[3]

As the cornerstone of Freud's insight, his theory of dreams came to occupy a paradoxical eminence.[4] Not only did Freud continue to value these early discoveries highly, he left the main features of his theory of dream interpretation relatively untouched, "essentially unaltered," in spite of major developments and revisions in fundamental aspects of his thinking.[5] And, as Jones states, his successors followed his lead in this. In David Hawkins's words, "Not only is it true that Freud himself did not subsequently revise the theory of dream processes but also that later psychoanalytic writers with few exceptions have had little to contribute. There are, of course, many papers dealing with dream interpretation and its use in psychoanalysis. These do not deal with the mechanism of the dream process, however."[6] At the same time, the combination of theoretical reverence and practical neglect was reflected in an apparently diminishing use of dream interpretation in psychoanalytic therapy, a trend that began during Freud's lifetime: "Freud often regretted that the interest in the technique and theory of dream-interpretation, instead of being kept in the fore of research where it belonged, was often bypassed by those who preferred their psychoanalysis easy and shallow. He used to say that he could judge the ability and psychological insight of an analyst best by seeing how he handled the interpretation of a dream."[7] Gregory Zilboorg's general comment on the development of psychoanalytic theory—"There are few, if any, among Freud's pupils or followers who made truly original contributions to that which has become known as psychoanalysis"—might have been applied to the theory of dream interpretation in particular.[8] In 1975 Leon Altman wrote a study with the specific intention of reviving interest in Freudian theory and correcting psychoanalytic neglect of dream interpretation as a major device in analysis.[9] Even more recently David Foulkes has commented that "Freud's *The Interpretation of Dreams* (1900) remains dream psychology's single most important work. . . . Freud's genius is best attested to by the fact, on the one hand, that subsequent empirical research rarely has been conducted without some direct influence of his views, and, on the other hand, that dream theory since 1900 has been, by and large, but a series of variations on Freud's early themes."[10] Thus the paradox: what was perhaps Freud's most important discovery remained undeveloped in his own theory and that of his followers and came to be de-emphasized as an analytic tool. The theory of dream interpretation stands, in psychoanalytic thinking, like a respected monument, a structure whose large contours have become familiar, but whose details have not been frequently reexamined.[11]

Freud's theory of dream interpretation gained and held its prominent position because the explanation of that theory suggested so many of Freud's key concepts. In its details and implications the theory is complicated, but perhaps we may settle on two general contributions which it made to our understanding of dreams: Freud showed that dreams are both meaningful and complex. By patiently exploring the complexity he found in them, he was able to trace their meaning back to the remote region of the unconscious. It was the relationship between the dream and this distant, underlying significance—the latent content—which gave the dream its meaning, however tortuous the chains of connection between the two. The complexity of the processes involved—the original processes of the dream's construction, as Freud saw them, and the processes of any relatively full Freudian analysis—has had its effect too, making the theory difficult to reexamine and evaluate thoroughly, but suggesting an intricacy of mental experience that serves in itself as the warrant for just such a reexamination.

It is at this point that the paradoxical status of Freud's theory of interpretation becomes significant for the work we have undertaken. Freud found a particular kind of meaning in dreams or, more precisely, by interpreting dreams; in order to establish that kind of meaning, the latent meaning, he had to sacrifice another. In effect, Freud found a meaning *behind* the dream at the price of the meaning *of* the dream. His theory required that any coherence of the manifest dream, the dream itself, be disregarded and rejected in order to discover the latent meaning. The complexity of mental life lay neither in the dream itself nor necessarily in the latent meaning behind it, but rather in the connections between the two. And the priority of latent meaning over manifest content dictated the method of interpretation—principally, that the manifest dream be regarded, not as a distinguishable entity, and certainly not as a coherent entity, but as a jumble of clues.[12] Freud's first and most basic principle of interpretation, therefore, requires the interpreter to separate the elements of the manifest dream, to fragment the surface that he finds, and to treat each of those elements as a distinct clue. At no point should the interpreter take the apparent integrity of a dream into account; those few dreams that seem obviously coherent on the surface are merely examples of a particular kind of disguise, and should be fragmented with a determination proportionate to their misleading appearance.[13] Once the latent meaning of the dream is revealed there is no occasion to refer it back to the manifest content or to try to place it in any relation to a coherent manifest order, for it is only the latent meaning which is being sought.

Freud's theory of dream interpretation, then, includes the principle that the manifest content of a dream is not coherent or, if it seems coherent, that this appearance has no significance. It will occur to the reader that if the manifest content were in any way coherent, Freud's strategy of interpretation would very effectively prevent the discovery of that unity. The methodology is based on his theoretical description of the dream processes, naturally enough. But the consequence of that dependence is that a psychoanalytic methodology is, by definition, incapable of answering the question, Is the dream itself coherent?

The title of Freud's great work was precisely chosen: he wrote about the interpretation of dreams and not about dreams themselves. The difference here is more than a quibble because the particular method of interpretation being proposed in Freud's theory defines and limits the phenomenon it purports to reveal. To put the matter another way, Freud wrote about dreams as *he* interpreted them. Because he was interested in dreams as a road to something else, he paid less attention to the road itself than he did to his destination and to the vehicle he had designed for his own transportation. The road acquired its significance from the use to which it could be put, not from its own characteristics. And precisely insofar as Freud's interpretive vehicle was designed to bring him to a particular destination, it was designed to exclude other destinations and to prevent an inspection of certain features of the thoroughfare.

Our first paradox—the neglected eminence of Freudian dream theory—must be joined by a second, therefore: Freud established the meaningfulness of dreams by construing them as incoherent in themselves. In combination, the two paradoxes have determined, to a remarkable degree, the limits of other dream theories and research. Because Freud's theory has been both prominent and unanalyzed (though not, of course, uncriticized), its built-in bias against the very possibility of manifest coherence has persisted, often unnoticed, in an influence that has touched nearly every succeeding consideration of the nature of dreams.

The New Science of Dreams

Implicit in David Foulkes's reference to "empirical research" is the second revolutionary development in the study of dreams in this century: the discovery of the correlation between Rapid Eye Movements and the occurrence of dreams which once again threw the whole topic of dreaming into the center of an energetic investigation. The important discovery of physiological indices to dreaming made a more clinical, scientific study of dreams seem possible, and sleep laboratories began producing a blizzard of specialized, precisely defined studies.[14] This work has often seemed to raise more questions than it could answer, but they have been interesting questions, and some of the clinical results have suggested the need for new attitudes towards the phenomenon of the dream. The mere confirmation of the frequency and regularity of dreaming (which Freud had surmised) and new speculation on its possible functions imply that the experience of dreaming is more than a psychic oddity or an inefficient and curiously elaborate "guardian of sleep." At the same time, the confirmation of this regularity and frequency gives a new piquancy to Freud's description of the dream as "a neurotic symptom, which, moreover, offers us the priceless advantage of occurring in all healthy people."[15] Furthermore, the high energy of this clinical activity has spilled over, encouraging new theorizing about the nature of dreams, their connections with other mental constructions, principally language, and their functions. An enormous amount of information has been and is being compiled. And yet, for all of their excitement and activity, the clinical studies have yielded a disappointingly small harvest of insight. Altman, for example, notes, "While recent research in sleep monitoring has turned up significant findings on the obligatory nature of dreaming, its length and recall, this research has not yielded information on the dream's content or formation."[16] Foulkes, after a review of major work in psychophysiological dream research, comes to exactly the same conclusion: "Despite the genuine advance some of the foregoing data represent in the search for better dream explanations, they have not led to any fundamentally new insight on crucial issues in dream psychology."[17] It seems that we know a great deal more about dreams in one sense but that the accumulating facts have not greatly improved our understanding of the essential nature of dreams. Something, apparently, is missing. In spite of the wealth of data and the exploratory attempts to connect dream theory to anthropological work (Róheim) or social psychology (Hall) or memory theory (Palombo) or linguistic theory (Edelson, Foulkes), and in spite of a fresh appreciation for the imaginative depth of dreams (Hillman, Rycroft)—in spite of the richness of these varied and various efforts, our understanding of the dream itself remains a colorful collection of starts and suggestions, of intriguing hints and thoughtful questions.

It is a curious and suggestive fact that a surprisingly large number of the studies published in the last twenty-five years are not really investigations of the dream itself. They are studies of the circumstances of dreaming, the patterns of dreaming, the psychological factors involved, the physiological or psychological causes, the functions, the sociology of dreaming, and so on. All of these inquiries, however valuable in themselves, are nonetheless oblique to the more fundamental question, What *is* a dream? And while those inquiries may yield helpful information and, on rare occasions, genuine insight into the nature of the dream, they do not address that fundamental question directly.

Because so much of the recent work has thus focussed on extremely limited features of the dream or on what we might call circumstantial aspects of the phenomenon, the influence of the Freudian paradoxes has continued. Freud's theories, as a more or less explicit bias, or at least as a point of reference, continue to influence the conceptions and preconceptions of current investigators, including many who consider themselves non-Freudian. It is amusing to see study after clinical study pursue painstakingly isolated topics and then make the most gratuitous references to Freud's theory—usually to the function of dreams as guardians of sleep or to their fulfillment of wishes—in order to relate the research at hand, however remotely, to established theory. This tendency gives some indication not only of the continuing influence of Freud's thinking, but also of the relative absence of alternate theorizing or even of serious reexamination of Freud's theorizing. If Freud established the significance of the dream at the price of its meaning, current laboratory work often attempts to establish one or another fact about dreaming at the price of its theoretical relevance. Thus the first paradox continues to reign: Freud's thinking persists as the unexamined, authoritative monument. Of particular interest to this study is the extent to which Freud's rejection of manifest coherence has operated as a silent assumption in more recent work, both clinical and theoretical. Even the content analysts, who specifically set aside all concern with latent meaning in order to concentrate on the manifest dream, have not confronted the question of an internal manifest coherence and have not, naturally, even begun to entertain the implications of such a possibility.[18] Freud's theory explicitly denigrated the manifest dream and denied it any significant coherence; his method of analysis, by definition, precluded any consideration of the possibility of manifest coherence. More recent researchers, although not bound to this theory and employing radically different methods of investigation, have nonetheless operated almost exclusively within the Freudian limits. The whole field has been governed by a bias which perfectly avoids the topic of internal manifest coherence.

In some ways all of this has helped to make the limits of Freudian dream theory more apparent. In the welter of new facts and questions it is even more clear that something essential is missing from our best understanding of the nature of the dream. Freud's main theses, transplanted from their native terrain, seem strangely vitiated of their explanatory power. Occasional glimpses of complex connections between a narrowly focussed clinical study and some detail of Freudian theory—Freud's description of one of the mechanisms of the dream-work, for example—hint that the Freudian monument includes largely unsuspected intricacies and, perhaps, gaps or omissions.

A survey of the current situation therefore suggests several interesting points. First of all, the shortcomings of both Freudian and more recent explanations of the dream and the consistent neglect of the possibility of manifest coherence encourage us to consider whether an examination of that possibility might not lead to new insight. Second, the monumental character of Freud's theory and its continued, though often silent, influence suggest that a reexamination of the phenomenon of dreaming centered on the question of manifest coherence might be most fruitfully conducted in relation to Freud's theory—the most comprehensive, detailed, and influential to date. Finally, there is a vague hint that the shortcomings of Freud's work and that of most recent investigators can be traced to a single blind spot and that in overlooking a single characteristic of the dream, Freud and his more recent successors have not only missed something essential, but have limited or biased all their thinking on the subject.

The Two Hypotheses

Our understanding of the dream is hampered by a single omission, traceable to Freud's work, which has fundamentally biased our thinking. We have overlooked one essential characteristic of the dream and, in so doing, have prevented ourselves from comprehending it. We have, that is, overlooked not only the fact of the dream's manifest coherence, but also the manner of that coherence, the basis of its unity. My purpose, therefore, is to investigate two simple hypotheses which, in conjunction, would correct this hiatus in our thinking about dreams:

1. The manifest dream, the dream itself, is an internally coherent psychic construction.
2. The mode of that internal coherence is aesthetic.

As simple as these hypotheses are, they have yet to receive serious attention, as the preceding survey has implied. Certainly both of them have been recognized in informal or metaphorical ways, in casual references and popular thinking. And it is true that, once they are clearly formulated, it is possible to see hints or suggestive implications of one or both of them in a number of recent studies.[19] But no major or detailed study has treated these hypotheses thoroughly. Much of the reason for that omission lies in the factors we have just been discussing; a second reason, however, lies in the nature of the hypotheses themselves. The first is untenable without the second, and the second poses particular difficulties for any investigator of dreams who cannot avail himself of an appropriate analytical method. Insofar as the dream is aesthetically unified it requires an aesthetic analysis, not a psychoanalytic or sociological analysis. Such approaches, because of their limited and quite different objectives and the concomitant limitations of their methodologies, cannot even investigate the possibility of an aesthetic dimension of dreaming. We are familiar with the procedure in which a psychologist or a sociologist examines a work of art and retrieves from it information valuable to his inquiry without taking into account the aesthetics of the work. We are also familiar with the results of such a procedure: the analyst may have discovered data of genuine value to his own discipline, but what he has to say tells us very little of the nature of the art object from which he has borrowed. Only an internal analysis employing the methodologies of literary or art criticism can reveal the essential nature of the work, even when the psychological or sociological insight is relevant to aesthetic function and must, therefore, be integrated into a full aesthetic analysis. We need to know the historical and sociological significance of, for example, the cup which Wealtheow offers Beowulf in the heroic poem; but we cannot appreciate the full significance of that cup in the dynamic of the literary work until we have considered its relationship to other features of the poem (e.g., the cup stolen from the dragon's hoard) in the manner of a literary analyst. The simple fact of the situation is that Freud and his varied successors have not had access to a methodology capable of addressing the question of aesthetic coherence in dreams.[20] Their procedures are no more capable of indicating the existence of an aesthetic dimension than a chemical analysis is capable of assessing the artistic qualities of an oil canvas.

If the dream possesses an aesthetic dimension, it requires an aesthetic analysis. If the elements and modes of coherence in the dream resemble, for example, the elements and modes of coherence in literary fiction, then we must analyze the dream in much the same way we would analyze a short story. We cannot explore the significance of any analogy between the dream and the short story without such an analysis. Obviously there are special difficulties for a literary analysis of dreams, beyond those involved in treating a short story or any formal work of art, and we may expect that those difficulties will require specific adjustments and qualifications. But, granting the obstacles to be overcome, we propose that an exploration of our two hypotheses will clarify an essential characteristic of the dream, one which has gone virtually untreated.

To say that a dream is coherent is not to say, however, that it is always intelligible. A short story in a foreign language may be thoroughly and deeply coherent and equally unintelligible. Any work of art which belongs to a new school, which is innovative and breaks with familiar traditions, may be based on a kind of coherence that cannot, at first, be understood by its audience. Misunderstandings of this sort have been a perennial phenomenon in the history of criticism of all the arts. To say that a dream is coherent, therefore, is merely to claim that the parts of the dream bear some relation to one another, that the distinguishable elements of the dream are *directly* related to each other. The hypothesis of coherence also implies that not only do the relationships among the elements of the dream pertain to whatever significance or meaning the dream might have, but that those relationships are a determinant of the dream's meaning. Thus, for example, if you dream that your father is driving a school bus across a sandy beach, the distinguishable elements of image, character, and setting are directly related to each other. This dream is somehow different from one in which your son drives the bus, or one in which your father drives a truck, or one in which the bus is being driven over narrow mountain roads rather than across a beach. The parts of the dream are related to one another and together constitute the dream as a distinguishable entity.

The relationships among these elements also determine whatever meaning the dream might have. The dream means one thing rather than another because it is a dream of your father; more specifically, however, it means something in particular about your father because he is driving a school bus and because he is driving it across a beach. It is clear, furthermore, that the meaningful relationships of elements such as these need not be limited to simple cases of combination or accumulation. These components do more than fit together like pieces of a jigsaw puzzle, side by side, in a cumulative configuration in which each of the separate elements retains a separate and static identity. In the dream composition it is quite possible that two elements influence and transform each other in their relationship, mutually conferring and determining each other's meanings. Thus the school bus may mean something quite distinct from what school buses ordinarily mean, precisely because it is being driven by your father, rather than someone else, across a beach, rather than somewhere else. Because the parts of the dream are related in this way, the dream constitutes a context for each of its parts, any of which may appear radically different outside of its dream context. We each have many fathers; only some of them drive school buses over beaches.

If the parts of the dream need to be considered in terms of their mutual relationships with one another, then both the parts themselves and the kinds of relationships they engage in require us to think of the mode of the dream's coherence as aesthetic. As the example above suggests, the elements which compose the dream are often definable in literary and dramatic terms; the dream deals in character, plot, setting, dialogue, imagery, symbolism, mood, tone, and, frequently enough, aesthetically functional structures. This point is so obvious that its implications are likely to be underestimated. But how is it that dreams happen to deal in the same materials that literary art manipulates? To what extent are the materials precisely similar? To the extent that they are really similar, shouldn't we consider exploring the parallels between dreams and literature by investigating the literary features of dreams rather than, as has been done so often, by examining the "dreamlike" (i.e., psychological) features of literature? How do Freud's standard categories of dream-work (condensation, displacement, plasticity, secondary revision) correlate with the literary categories into which the same dream features might be placed? Finally, if the elements which compose dreams resemble the devices which compose works of literature, might not the coherence of the compositions also be similar? If literary elements exist in dreams, perhaps they behave like literary elements there.[21]

No dreamer or student of dreams, of whatever theoretical orientation, would deny that many of the elements of dreams somehow resemble those of literature. Certainly the scholarship on dreams, beginning with Freud's, is peppered with casual comparisons and informal metaphors. Such and such a dream is like a drama, or a little tragedy, or a comedy. This dream has a vivid setting while that one has a complicated plot. The mood of this dream was tranquil, or terrifying; the tone of that one seemed ironic. Once we pause to take these easy analogies seriously, however, we are brought to the question which marks an entirely different approach to the subject and which raises further questions close on its heels, as we have seen. It is clear, even from a cursory summary of Freudian theory, how radically this approach differs from Freud's; we can only guess—since his dream theory occupies such a strategic position in his larger psychology—how far-reaching the implications of that difference might turn out to be.

As a matter of fact, however, no reader of dreams succeeds in ignoring manifest coherence altogether, even in the effort of producing a purely Freudian interpretation of a purely latent content. Freud himself, in spite of his unvarying proscription against the procedure, frequently makes silent use of congruences in the manifest dream in order to construct his interpretation of latent meaning, as we will see at first hand in the following pages. His practice frequently violates his theory. And while more recent students of the dream have yet to explore the hypothesis of manifest coherence, much of their work indirectly implies its plausibility.

It is also true that developments in both literary and visual arts in the twentieth century (and parallel developments in the criticism and theory of those arts) have made the hypothesis of aesthetic coherence in dreams easier to consider. If the dream at first appears incoherent because it is so unrealistic, or because it juxtaposes unexpected elements, or because its major sections seem surprisingly disjointed, or because it uses imagery and symbols that seem to carry intricate, private, and perhaps thoroughly idiosyncratic significances, we need only think of analogous devices and strategies purposely cultivated in the contemporary arts to realize that the aesthetic dimension of the dream is a subject ripe for investigation. And we may expect contemporary literature and the visual arts to offer a range of helpful analogies and specific models for that investigation. In a sense, the dream stands at a powerful juncture of converging trends. Even more than Freud suspected it is a normal and frequent experience of the individual psyche, and it relates to crucial issues of Freudian and non-Freudian psychology on the one hand, and to some of the most interesting and varied developments of the arts on the other.

The Test

In beginning an exploration of the two proposed hypotheses, I have chosen a particular strategy, one which seemed appropriate to the hypotheses themselves and to the theoretical terrain on which I wished to engage them. It seemed important to address the hypotheses against a Freudian background, given the situation of dream theory just described. Freud's thought is obviously complex, however, and the attempt to relate these two hypotheses to the intricacies of his dream theory alone would be a large undertaking. It seemed more advisable to make an initial presentation by means of a practical demonstration rather than a broad theoretical construction. I was mindful, too, of how often applications or critiques of Freud's theories hover at a given level of generality, assuming or ignoring subordinate levels of detail that, in fact, contradict the generalities. It is perplexing, for example, to see Calvin Hall denounce the Freudian concept of latent meaning on one page of an article and then, a few pages later in the same study, proceed to endorse Freud's description of the dream-work—which is, after all, nothing but a description of the relationships between latent and manifest content.[22]

In order to present these hypotheses, therefore, I have chosen a single, extended example as a test case. The example is a strategic one, without question, and since it is drawn from one of Freud's case histories, it offers an opportunity for detailed treatment that no specimen in *The Interpretation of Dreams* or, for that matter, any other work of Freud's can offer. My practical implementation of an analysis based on the two hypotheses of manifest coherence constantly raises theoretical questions, of course, and I am well aware that the discussion in the following chapters frequently implies the need for a complementary theoretical exposition. It seemed best to postpone that work, though, in order to guard the clarity of this demonstration, even though the depth and concentrated detail of this analysis might temporarily distract the reader from the breadth of its implications. I have used the last chapter to sketch out the general range of those implications in a very rough way. The main work here, however, is an aesthetic analysis of a single dream, as thorough as I have been able to make it. It will, I hope, lay a secure footing for later theoretical work.

Chapter Two

The Art of Dora's Dream

The Elements of the Dream

If we were to seek a specific and detailed example upon which to illustrate the contrasts and relationships between a Freudian interpretation of a dream and an aesthetic reading, we could not do better than choose the famous case history of Dora.[1] This first of Freud's case histories, composed within a year of the publication of *The Interpretation of Dreams*, was closely connected with that work in Freud's mind; in his prefatory remarks he explains that "the title of the work was originally 'Dreams and Hysteria,' for it seemed to me peculiarly well-adapted for showing how dream-interpretation is woven into the history of a treatment and how it can become the means of filling in amnesias and elucidating symptoms" (*Dora*, p. 10). A page later he comments again that "the case history before us seems particularly favored as regards the utilization of dreams," and in a letter to Wilhelm Fliess written on January 25, 1901, the day after he finished composing the case history, he refers to it as "a fragment of an analysis of a hysteria, in which the interpretations are grouped round two dreams, so it is really a continuation of the dream book."[2] Ernest Jones repeats this last phrase in his brief description of the work and explains how the case history's emphasis on the connection between dreams and psychoneurotic symptoms complements the final chapter in *The Interpretation of Dreams*, which did not deal with psychopathology: "One sees, therefore, that the Dora analysis is really a continuation of *The Interpretation of Dreams*.

It centers on two main dreams which are analyzed at length in a way that beautifully illustrates the interconnection between them and the patient's sufferings. The essay is especially instructive from the point of view of technique, both in the analytic procedure itself and in the therapeutic handling of the case."[3]

The "Fragment of an Analysis of a Case of Hysteria," therefore, can be seen as an extension, a demonstration by actual application, of Freud's theories of the dream.[4] Frank Sulloway elaborates on the theoretical role of the case history, following Jones's suggestion:

> [In *The Interpretation of Dreams*, Freud] found it expedient to rely heavily upon his own dreams—a decision that was not without its own dilemma, for he could not interpret his own dreams fully without revealing considerably more of himself to the public than he reasonably cared to do. . . . The upshot was that Freud used parts of his dream interpretations to reveal different aspects of his theory but nowhere elected to reveal, as he himself confessed, the complete or ultimate meaning of any of his own dreams. . . . Freud apparently believed he could overcome these various omissions from his argument by writing a concluding chapter to *The Interpretation of Dreams* entitled "Dreams and the Neuroses." This chapter would have allowed Freud to give a full and ruthless analysis of several patients' dreams. . . . Freud's proposed chapter on dreams and neurosis was never written. . . . the theoretical gap created by this important omission in Freud's argument was later filled by two separate publications: the "Dora" case history . . . and the *Three Essays on the Theory of Sexuality* . . .[5]

In the same vein, Steven Marcus writes that the case history "was to be nothing less than a concentrated synthesis of Freud's first two major works, *Studies on Hysteria* (1895) and *The Interpretation of Dreams* (1900), to which there had been added the new dimension of the 'sexual-organic basis,' that is, the psychosexual developmental stages that he was going to represent in fuller detail in the *Three Essays on the Theory of Sexuality* (1905). It was thus a summation, a new synthesis, a crossing point and a great leap forward all at once."⁶

Thus, because the case history of Dora could present a much more detailed and nearly complete analysis of two dreams, it could make clear the important connection Freud wished to establish between dreams and symptoms.⁷ In this enterprise Freud is credited with success. Despite certain limitations in the material, Jones claims, "this beautiful little monograph" is characterized by "confident penetration"; Sulloway concludes that "through the 'Dora' case history, the theory of dreams blends inextricably into the theory of sexuality"; Philip Rieff, in a spirited introduction to the text, praises the "sheer brilliance which is still breath-taking"; and Steven Marcus speaks of "pages of dazzling originality, of creative genius performing with compactness, complexity, daring, and splendor that seem close to incomparable in their order."⁸

The limitations are not trivial, however, and they relate directly to the dream analyses in the case. Dora's analysis was not a success—she left treatment after only eleven weeks—and the dreams, particularly the second, which she reported to Freud only a few days before her sudden announcement that she was terminating, address themselves to this topic. Not only do the dreams treat the topic of Dora's termination in itself, they also comment on the reason for the failure of the analysis, a certain difficulty in the transference.⁹ Freud recognized this topicality of the dreams and he readily admits mishandling the transference, but he is unable to explain, in convincing detail, the precise difficulty in the transference or the relation of the dreams to that complication. This situation makes Dora's second dream a particularly intriguing test case for our comparison of aesthetic and Freudian interpretations because it suggests an especially vivid point of comparison between the two approaches: as we will see, the aesthetic reading introduces new information and offers an explanation, not only of Freud's shortcomings in his dream analyses, but also of his mishandling of the transference and of Dora's motives for sabotaging the analysis.

In order to render the contrast between the two methods of interpretation as lucid and exact as possible, it will be best to proceed in stages. First, in this chapter, we will examine Dora's second dream by itself, without reference to any biographical information or any interpretation of Freud's.[10] This tactic will yield an obviously limited understanding of the dream, but one which will clearly distinguish the observable features of the manifest dream, separating them out from the amalgamation of manifest elements, associations, biographical facts, and interpretations of latent elements which combine in Freud's presentation. As we will see, this limited first approach can easily establish the scope and nature of the dream's aesthetic dimension and can even sketch the major features of a comprehensive interpretation, one which can then be compared to the facts of the case history for verification. Subsequent chapters will make that comparison after first summarizing the background and explaining (and extending) Freud's interpretation; the last step will be to apply the insights generated by our aesthetic reading to the problem of the transference and the failure of the analysis.[11]

Let us turn directly to Dora's second dream, then; the text is this:

> *I was walking about in a town which I did not know. I saw streets and squares which were strange to me. [I saw a monument in one of the squares.] Then I came into a house where I lived, went to my room, and found a letter from Mother lying there. She wrote saying that as I had left home without my parents' knowledge she had not wished to write to me to say that Father was ill. "Now he is dead, and if you like [?] you can come."*
>
> *I then went to the station ("Bahnhof") and asked about a hundred times: "Where is the station?" I always got the answer: "Five minutes." I then saw a thick wood before me which I went into, and there I asked a man whom I met. He said to me: "Two and a half hours more [or, two hours]." He offered to accompany me. But I refused and went alone. I saw the station in front of me and could*

not reach it. *At the same time I had the usual feeling of anxiety that one has in dreams when one cannot move forward.*

Then I was at home. I must have been travelling in the meantime, but I know nothing about that. I walked into the porter's lodge, and enquired for our flat. The maidservant opened the door to me and replied that Mother and the others were already at the cemetery ("Friedhof"). [After she had answered I went to my room, but not the least sadly (or, calmly), and began reading a big book that lay on my writing-table.] [I saw myself particularly distinctly going up the stairs.] (Dora, p. 94, divisions added) [12]

The three scenes are distinctly separate. In the first Dora is in "a town which I did not know," and it is here that she finds the letter announcing her father's death. In direct response to this news she changes scenes, moving into the second one—"I then went to the station"—which is vague except for the thick woods and the station itself, when she finally sees it. After a sudden transition, Dora finds herself in the third and last scene, at home.

The scenes differ in composition, in the style of their presentation, in the fact that, as a sequence, they establish a chronology, and in other respects as well.[13] The first and third scenes are distinct and comprehensible except for the specific paradoxes in each. In the first scene Dora does not know the town even though she lives there and locates her room without apparent difficulty. The third scene contrasts directly with this: although Dora is home, rather than in a strange town, she must inquire about her flat as though she were unable to find it or did not have direct access to it. The juxtaposition is perfectly symmetrical: an unknown place containing an accessible room is balanced by a known place containing an inaccessible room.

In contrast, the middle scene is confusing and "dreamlike" throughout.[14] Dora goes to the station but has to ask where it is; when she does ask, she is given the answer in terms of time rather than in directions; again, the times change inexplicably from five minutes to two and a half hours, as if she were getting farther away from rather than nearer her goal; and when she finally sees the station "in front of me," she cannot reach it. The main idea of the middle section is movement, travel between the static locations of the first and third scenes; but Dora's movement is either undirected or frozen. There is a certain structural irony to this, since both the first and last sections concern travel too: in each of them Dora travels "locally," on foot, in order to return to a home; and each of them begins with this movement of return and concludes with an image of Dora stationary, reading. In the first section she is "walking about" (Freud later paraphrases this as "wandering about"), apparently without a particular destination, as if casually sight-seeing. "Then I came into a house where I lived": Dora arrives at a destination ("*a* house"), but it is not clear whether she has chosen to return there or has stumbled across it, perhaps even unexpectedly, in her walking. In the middle section this situation is exactly reversed; Dora knows precisely where she wants to go but cannot find the station, in spite of asking directions "about a hundred times." When she finally does see the station before her, her movements are frozen. Then in the third section, the situation is a combination of the first two. As in the town scene Dora walks freely and returns to her room but, as in the middle section, she has a specific destination from the beginning and must inquire in order to reach it. Also, she is more conscious of her movement near the end of the dream (as she was conscious of her paralysis in the middle)—she sees herself going up the stairs "particularly distinctly."

In another sense, however, Dora is dislocated in all three of the scenes, though in different ways. In the first scene she is not at home, but "in a town which I did not know," and so she is not present during her father's sickness or at the event of his death. In the second scene she is not at the station, in spite of her attempts to reach it. In the last scene she is not at the cemetery. In different ways, Dora is absent from the main site of the action each time, and her own actions form a plot of counterpoint to that other, offstage plot. In this respect, too, the middle section is contrapuntal because in it she tries to arrive at the site, and the section as a whole concerns her travel home, back to the displaced site of the first scene. The function of the whole section is duplicated or echoed in its specific plot, of course, which concerns Dora's local travel to the station, the immediate journey she must make in order to commence her larger journey home. The structure in this respect is something like a pair of Chinese boxes. On the local level, she is unsuccessful: she never arrives at the station. This would seem to make the larger trip impossible but, mysteriously, the larger journey is successful (*"Then* I was at home. I must have been travelling in the meantime, but I know nothing about that"). In contrast to this middle section, where Dora's local destination eludes her, in the first and last sections she intentionally avoids the site of the important action: in the first scene she is away from home because she left without her parents' knowledge, as if she were avoiding the scene of her father's death (that is certainly the result of her leaving home); in the last scene she does not go to the cemetery.

Almost as important in the dream as the sense of place, and the composition of related scenes and the emphasis on travel among them, is the subject of time. That topic appears at different levels in the dream and is also developed through the sonata-like structure of the scenes. At the beginning Dora is too late for her father's death, and at the end she is too late for his burial ("the others were already at the cemetery"). In the middle section, however, she is, in a peculiar way, too early. Her distance from the station is always measured in time, and she is not yet there ("five minutes"; "two and a half hours more") until the end of the section, when she cannot get there. But the reversal is more intricate than this; when she asks the man in the woods, he tells her that the station is now two and a half hours away, rather than the five minutes it had been—she is even "earlier" than she was at the beginning of the section. Finally, when she sees the station she cannot reach it, and she seems caught in a dreamlike stasis in which time has stopped altogether. It is almost as if each section were running on a different clock.[15] In the first and third scenes the clocks are similar, but in the middle scene the clock runs backwards and then stops altogether.

At a different level, time functions as a structural principle demarcating the scenes. Their order is chronological, and Dora travels from one scene to the next by crossing a chronological border in each instance: "I *then* went to the station"; "*Then* I was at home." Chronological order is the simplest, of course, in a dream or a story. But here the device is made more prominent than it need be ("then" occurs four times in the dream, in addition to "now," "always," "at the same time," "in the meantime," "already," and "after"), and it acquires a certain interest, or at least suspiciousness, because of the structural "time zones" in the dream, because of the unexpected substitution of times for distances in the middle section, and because time seems to be an important theme in the dream. The question is whether the chronological structure is itself thematic.

Finally, time operates in a very specialized way in the middle section of the dream. Not only does Dora receive answers expressed in time instead of distance but the particular times may be in some way symbolic. The two specific figures are made noticeable by their odd function and enigmatic suggestiveness as well as by the rhetoric of their presentation: the first time, "five minutes," is repeated "about a hundred times," and the second answer is doubly surprising and mysterious. That second figure is even more suspicious because, in repeating the dream, Dora changed it from "two and a half hours" to "two hours," the only alteration (in contrast to the additions) which her several addenda made to the text.

In addition to these important themes of travel and time—themes closely related in the dream as they can so easily be—a third major theme is prominent, that of information and knowledge. In a sense it is the keynote of the dream, for the first two sentences announce and emphasize this topic: "I was walking about in a town which *I did not know*. I saw streets and squares *which were strange to me*." Next, Dora returns to her room in the house where she is living and this seems to be familiar, to be known to her, in spite of the fact that it is located in the unknown town. The first scene culminates with a further development of the theme: the letter from Dora's mother conveys the knowledge of her father's death. This discovery is set against the background fact that Dora had left home without her parents' knowledge—in fact, Dora's mother cites that circumstance as her reason for not informing Dora of her father's illness ("as I had left home without my parents' knowledge she had not wished to write to me to say that Father was ill"). The symmetry is perfectly neat and connects this theme to those of travel and time: Dora has travelled away from knowledge in leaving her home for the unknown town and now can travel back home after receiving the knowledge that her father is dead. *Now* she can return home.

In the second section Dora energetically seeks knowledge but she encounters difficulties; she repeats her initial inquiry a hundred times and receives answers that seem more confusing than enlightening. The situation is doubly confusing because Dora is travelling about in search of the information she needs in order to travel home. Then when she finds the station she still cannot reach it; both time and movement stop.

The third section opens by echoing the particular motif of the first. Dora is at home, but does not know how she travelled there—the transition has been purely chronological. In this case, however, her ignorance is not inconvenient, just as it was not in the first section where she found her room although she did not know the town. Then, once she is home, Dora's first action is to travel in order to make an inquiry ("I walked into the porter's lodge, and enquired for our flat"). The final result of this inquiry is not only access to the flat, but the knowledge that her mother and the others are already at the cemetery and that she is, in a sense, too late. Dora concludes the dream by travelling upstairs in order to read the big book, a source of knowledge.

Thus time, travel, and knowledge weave their way through the dream like three braided strands, now one and now another showing foremost, but none of them ever disappearing entirely, and each of them in constant contact with the others. The knowledge of her father's death (his time is up) spurs Dora to travel, but her journey is impeded by a lack of information until she finds herself at home, without journeying there, and finds that she is too late, whereupon she travels upstairs to read her big book.

Two other elements seem to develop coherently through the design of the manifest dream, and both of them are most easily explained in terms of the structure of the dream. One of these elements is a sequence of images which function something like landmarks for Dora. In the unknown town she sees "a monument in one of the squares." This monument—the only singularized and specific image in the first scene other than the letter—immediately suggests and links two of the ideas which dominate the dream, the idea of time and that of her father's death. The ideas reappear in the third section, more obviously though less visually, in the reference to the cemetery where Dora's dead father will, presumably, be memorialized by a monument. The corresponding image in the middle section is, as usual, of a different order: there the train station stands out as the landmark of that particular geography. In some respects the station seems to counterpoint the bracketing monuments of the beginning and end of the dream: a station is the site of the beginning of a journey, not its end (monument, cemetery); it is the place Dora is unable to reach (we are all able to reach the cemetery); and it is the beginning of the journey that would return her to the home her father is leaving. In other respects, however, the station is connected with the two monuments between which it stands: Dora seeks the station in response to the news of her father's death, and when she sees the station, time stands still, as it does for a monument. A connection between train travel and death would not be unprecedented; in speaking of typical dreams Freud said, "Dreams of missing a train . . . are dreams of consolation for another kind of anxiety felt in sleep—the fear of dying. 'Departing' on a journey is one of the commonest and best authenticated symbols of death."[16] Whether these implications are useful in understanding Dora's dream remains to be established, but their topicality is certainly suggestive.

In addition to the settings, themes, and images, we should also consider the symmetrical orchestration of the dream's small cast of characters throughout its three segments. The characters are disposed within two sequences of pairs, each of which develops progressively in the dream. Dora forms one of the pair in every case, and the first sequence matches her with her absent father in the first section, the man in the woods in the middle section, and her absent father again in the last section. Her father's absence (death) is so important in the first and last parts that it has the influence of a kind of negative image, a vacuum which is nearly palpable. When these absences are placed on either side of the solitary appearance of the man in the woods, the effect is something like a reversal of figure and ground. In this detail as in every other we have encountered thus far, the middle element is contrapuntal and transitional: the man in the woods gives Dora directions for her journey from one paternal absence (her father in another town) to another (her father in the cemetery). The parallelism poses immediate questions about the man in the woods, of course.

The second, or alternate, sequence of pairs joins Dora with her mother (via the letter) in the first scene, Dora with the man in the woods again in the middle scene, and Dora with the maidservant in the final scene. In this sequence the thread of continuity is that each character delivers information to Dora. There seems to be a middle reversal in this sequence too, in its female-male-female pattern and in its relative-stranger-servant pattern. There may also be something of a progressive decline in the status of the characters (mother-guide-servant) as well as in the importance of the information they convey. It is very noticeable, of course, that the man in the woods figures in both sequences, and we may wonder whether his double role is the dream's way of relating the two sequences to each other by using him as a kind of junction.

We may close this survey of the formal features of Dora's dream by returning once more to the topic of structure in order to make a more detailed observation, one that might seem overdone were the dream's organization less controlled than it has turned out to be. Clearly, structural effects are central to this dream, and this last refinement of our earlier description will deepen our impression of their intricacy. The main characteristic of the superstructure is the division of the dream into three distinct scenes, the first and last of which parallel each other and bracket a contrasting middle. Each of these three sections is further subdivided and the structures themselves enact the sonatalike pattern already noticed. Furthermore, each of these subsections is demarcated in exactly the same way as the three major scenes, by a chronological reference. Thus the first scene is divided into two parts, Dora's walk around the strange town and her reading of her mother's letter in her room; the transition is signalled by "then": "Then I came into a house where I lived, went to my room, and found a letter from Mother lying there." In the last scene of the dream the subdivision is exactly parallel. First Dora walks into the porter's lodge and makes her inquiries; in the second subsection she again goes to her room to read, and here too the transition is signalled by a chronological reference: "After she had answered I went to my room." The middle section employs a different local structure; it is subdivided into three parts rather than two and that in itself distinguishes it from the other two scenes on purely structural grounds. In the first subsection of the middle scene Dora asks where the station is. In the second subsection she enters the woods and receives a different answer from the man she meets. In the third subsection she sees the station before her but cannot reach it. Here, too, chronological references separate the subdivisions; the second begins with "I then saw a thick wood before me" and the last begins with "I saw the station in front of me and could not reach it. At the same time . . ."

This level of structural detail is interesting for two reasons. In the first place, it reinforces our growing impression of the dream as a completed and intricate production and in so doing justifies our interest in its details. The dream seems precise enough to repay the kind of specific analysis we have been applying to it. The second intriguing aspect of the detailed structure is this: since the dream is so thoroughly ordered, the order itself must be considered a major element of its style. Its formality must be accounted for. This naturally leads to the question of how to read the dream's structure even on the major level. Is the movement in the dream linear or circular, progressive or ritualistically static? Is the third scene a development of the first two or is it a formal restatement of the first?

Finally, the details of the structure suggest the possibility that the dream may be self-reflective. In discussing the theme of time we noted the possibility that chronology might be considered as both form and content, structure and also subject matter. If that is so, then the dream is partly about itself. The same potential exists in the structural elaborations we have been discussing. What, for example, is the relationship between the three-part superstructure and the three-part local structure of the middle section? Does the middle section simply repeat and echo the formal principle on a different scale, or does it comment, by means of the structural analogy, on the dream as a whole?

Questions like this last one indicate clearly how far we have been able to come and what remains ahead. We have made a very definite kind of progress even though we have been looking at the dream exclusively, without benefit of background or context of any sort. Even at this point we know something about this dream which Freud did not know and was not interested in considering. We know that it employs a variety of "literary" devices, manipulates them with apparent consistency, and seems to harmonize them with each other. This in itself is a significant observation, for it suggests some degree of artistry in the manifest dream and a kind and level of manifest coherence which has never received thorough investigation.

Nevertheless, we do not know what the dream means and, until we do, we obviously cannot assess this aesthetic dimension completely. It is one thing to claim that a manifest dream text includes literary devices such as setting and imagery and quite another thing to claim that the dream generates meaning through those devices. In the final analysis, it is the harmony of those elements at the manifest level which we cannot assess without determining the meaning of the dream for, if the manifest dream is an aesthetic production, its meaning lies precisely in the significant cooperation and mutual influence of those elements. At this stage we have little more than a catalogue of features; we need to determine whether they also form a composition.

In order to do that we might, of course, turn to the facts of the case, the rich context for the dream which Freud has applied in the case history. It would not be difficult to relate the observations we have made to the specifics of Dora's situation. Much of the private language of her individual psyche would become available to us and we could use that knowledge for an aesthetic "translation" of the dream. But it will better serve our purpose to wait, to delay that advantage just a while longer. What if the dream, this dream at least, is capable of communicating meaning even without the benefit of its context? If the mere text of the dream, innocent of facts, history, associations, and interpretations, can speak coherently, then surely our interest in its aesthetic dimension will be justified. And at that point we can compare our purely aesthetic reading to the facts of the case as well as to Freud's interpretation in order to understand precisely what contribution the aesthetic reading can make.

A Reading of the Dream

If we are to specify significances and resolve ambiguities for the elements we have discovered in the manifest text, we can only do that by relating them more cogently to one another. In any aesthetic production meaning is *composed* before it is communicated, and in the order of a composition individual elements support, limit, and alter their significances; in so doing, they mutually confer meaning upon one another.

Our review of the formal features of the dream suggests that its themes are central. The characters are simple and even Dora is not highly developed (though there are significant changes in her dream character, as we will see). The setting, imagery, tone, and plot are also relatively simple; none of them has the power to dominate and order all the other elements. And while the structure of the dream is elaborate and essential, we cannot appreciate its value until we know more precisely what is being structured.

Of the three topics weaving throughout the dream, the theme of knowledge is the deepest and most likely to dominate. The ideas of travel and time—so easily related to each other as they are here—serve a more literal function and a more limited one. The dream, then, is a story about information and knowledge. In the beginning Dora is living in a strange environment, a town she does not know, and she has come to it without her parents' knowledge. That circumstance suggests several possibilities. Most literally, Dora has chosen to avoid her parents' scrutiny; she has done something she did not want them to know about—perhaps she was able to do it only because they did not know about it. What she did was leave her parents, that is, she made herself independent of them. But another implication may be pertinent: Dora left home without the benefit of her parents' knowledge, lacking their capabilities. In some way she lacks experience or understanding that might be helpful to her. Thus the town is strange, and she tours this new landscape as if examining it; she reads the town, and then returns to her room to read the information in her mother's letter.

The letter is an obvious vehicle of information and suggests a third implication of Dora's having left "without her parents' knowledge": since she left, she has had no knowledge of them. The letter brings such knowledge and makes clear, too, that her father is the key figure involved in all these considerations. Now that he is dead she "can" return home if she chooses. It must have been her father's scrutiny in particular which she was avoiding, and it is clearly knowledge of her father which she has especially lacked and which the letter conveys. And, probably, it is particularly her father's knowledge (experience, understanding) which she lacks in the strange town.

Dora reads the letter and sets out for home immediately. But returning is not easy, even though the necessary prerequisite, her father's death, has been satisfied. She needs information, directions to the station, and the answers to her inquiries seem inappropriate and unhelpful. When Dora enters the thick woods she seems to be losing ground, in a sense, entering a landscape more remote and primitive than the world of towns and trains, and a landscape where it might be even easier to lose one's way. The anonymous man she meets there offers his help, but his reply to her inquiry is no more comprehensible than the earlier ones. In fact, it is discouraging because Dora now seems farther away from the station. But she chooses to continue, alone. Finally she sees the station, though it is not clear how the communication she received ("two and a half hours more") helped or hindered her. When she does find the station, however, it is clear that she requires additional intelligence, for she cannot reach it even though it is now before her. It seems, at this moment in the dream, that Dora will not be able to return home because she has not been able to acquire the information she needs for the journey, or because the information she has been seeking is not to the point.

She does return home, of course, but without knowing how. The transition is unexplained, a simple transition in time, and in this respect it repeats her experience in searching for the station. Once she is home, it becomes apparent that she has not returned to either her father or her mother, but to her own room.[17] If Dora has had a specific objective in returning home, it can only have been her own room and the book she reads there. The book is obviously a source of knowledge, and so Dora's story about knowledge ends in her finding this source. What exactly the book represents we cannot determine from the text alone. It is in some way important, clearly, because it is big; it is in some way private or personal, because it is in Dora's room; it is ironically situated on her writing table and so she reads instead of writes (. . . letters? a letter brought her here); and it is somehow connected with her father's death, since that event allowed her to come home to it, and since she chooses to read the book rather than go to the cemetery. She is reading it "without her parents' knowledge," certainly, and probably in all three senses. But it is not clear whether the knowledge she seeks in the big book pertains directly to her father's death, or whether that event was merely a necessary prerequisite to her investigation of some other subject.

In either case, the final image in the dream recalls the opening scene very particularly, and so helps to explain the result of Dora's quest. At the end, in a familiar setting rather than a strange one, Dora walks up the stairs (instead of walking about a town), reads the big book instead of her mother's letter, and chooses to read that book instead of visiting her father's monument (and instead of seeing the monument in the square at the beginning). Dora has succeeded at least in replacing one kind of search with another, and she has emphatically escaped "her parents' knowledge" in order to seek (or in the course of seeking) her own knowledge, even though she does not know the details of her transition.

The level of knowledge which Dora needs or seeks, and her relative success in finding it, are tempered at every stage by the influence of time. Since the dream has dealt with this topic so prominently and at different levels (as a structural device; as a literal topic in the middle scene; as a theme in itself), we naturally turn to its bearing on Dora's quest for knowledge. Is she moving forwards or backwards in time as the dream progresses? To what extent do changes in time imply changes in the content of the knowledge she seeks (or in the circumstances in which she seeks it, or in the methods by which she seeks it, or in her success), and to what extent is time itself the subject of her search, the topic about which Dora seeks knowledge?

On its literal level the story of the dream advances chronologically, of course, but that does not necessarily imply that the character also progresses chronologically in all respects. In one sense, at least, Dora goes backwards as the time of the dream goes forwards: she returns home to the setting and perhaps the concerns of a period that is earlier than the unknown town of the beginning. The paradox also applies to her relationship with her father: after his time has advanced to its forward limit, Dora is free to move backwards, to an earlier phase of her own time. On the one hand, she has outlived her father; but on the other hand, she has returned to the setting of her youth. She becomes metaphorically younger and older when (or because) her father has become older and has died. This same paradox emerges on the literal level in the second section of the dream: as Dora progresses towards the elusive station (in terms of the plot's chronology), the time which separates her from the station increases. And when she is geographically near it, time freezes and the separation in time becomes static, or infinite.

In other ways, too, Dora's passage through time is paradoxical.

At the end of the dream she reads the big book rather than the letter she had read in the first section. Whatever the exact contents of the book, it is older than her mother's letter, which brought current news. And she reads at her writing table, after her mother has written her but before she has written anything—she reads instead of writing. Each reference to time and each image or action that contributes to the temporal network of the dream suggests the same question: is Dora moving forwards or backwards in time, or is she, ultimately, standing still?

The answer lies in the middle section, both in its details and in its larger function in the structure of the dream. The details make the topic of time explicit: in this section Dora's movement forwards has the effect of pulling her backwards (from "five minutes" to "two and a half hours" away) until she is frozen in front of the station and time stops altogether. Within this section the plot moves forwards even as the clock runs backwards; it seems we must answer our question by saying that Dora moves *both* forwards and backwards in time. This fits the function of the section as a whole, too, since it serves as a transition from the first scene to the third, that is, from the future to the past in one sense, and from the past into the future in another sense. The dream is a journey and Dora's destination, the home she returns to, is both future and past: it is later than the first scene in the chronology of the plot, but it represents an earlier period in the sense that Dora finally resumes an earlier part of herself. Dora's future lies in her past—in wish, fantasy, or fact.

The middle section not only functions as a transition, however; it also treats the very idea of transition and explains how Dora is to make her paradoxical progress. Thus the section climaxes in the anxious paralysis which overcomes Dora directly in front of the station. Her progress (backwards and forwards) is stopped; she is unable to advance. But when the next section begins she *has* advanced; she has completed the paradoxical progress which was dramatized and then frozen in the middle section. Time, it seems, is not only Dora's destination but her vehicle as well. Thus the perplexing directions she receives in the middle section are precisely accurate: Dora can move from one place to another only through time, by means of time. There is no other form of transportation at her disposal but, the dream tells her, no other is necessary. Time will move her, unpredictably and incomprehensibly, into a future which includes her past. In a sense, time will move her towards the study of time itself, Dora's study of herself and her past.

The station, the controlling image of the middle section, embodies these paradoxical themes. Its very presentation is paradoxical: it is made prominent by its absence, and once it is found, it cannot be reached. It is a starting point for travel but, within the section, functions as a destination. It perfectly embodies the idea of transition, of course, and it is the only thing in the dream which provokes an emotional reaction from Dora. Naturally, the one fact explains the other. What Dora searches for and cannot find is a device or mode of transition; when she does find it, after meeting the man in the woods, she is overcome with anxiety. Her anxiety is provoked by the idea of change which the station represents. She seeks the station and yet is frightened by it; when she is nearest to it she is least capable of reaching it. Here again is the familiar paradoxical style of the dream, and it is easy to relate Dora's ambivalence towards the station to her ambivalence towards her father, herself, and the themes of time and knowledge. The station is a compact and intense center of paradox: the very fact that Dora needs to ask directions to it is odd (how had she travelled to the unknown town?), her progress towards it is strange, and her finding of it is equally problematical. When she sees it she is unable to reach it; then she is suddenly home as if she never needed to make use of the station in the first place.[18]

This clarifies our understanding of the themes of time and knowledge in the dream by developing the third theme, that of travel. Of the several possible relationships among these themes, the dream proposes and emphasizes one in particular. Time and travel are not parallel, as we might expect them to be, nor is knowledge the simple fruit of travel. Rather, travel in the dream is entirely metaphorical, and its function is to express the relationship between time and knowledge. It is a metaphor rather than a theme, as it had seemed to be. The gist of the metaphor is that time, in and of itself, will effect a change in the circumstances and objectives of Dora's quest for knowledge. Time is the mode of travel available, and the destination is not only another time (a future including the past) but a different knowledge based in that new time. The metaphor also makes clear that the knowledge which Dora so actively sought in the middle section, knowledge about how to make the journey or transition, is not essential—Dora arrives "knowing nothing about that."

The main insight of the dream on the relationship between time and knowledge is twofold. The third section makes the statement that time generates knowledge (or at least it allows the quest for knowledge) in two distinct ways. First of all, time passes, suddenly and without depending on a decision on Dora's part, and without regard for her anxiety: "Then I was at home." The mere fact that such a transition can occur is important knowledge for Dora. Secondly, once the leap forward has occurred, Dora is free to pursue the knowledge of the big book. The fact that time itself is the vehicle for Dora's progress and that it is, in a sense, out of her control, is reassuring, given her experience of the paralyzing anxiety of the middle section. The dream, finally, offers knowledge about the way time leads to knowledge. It both employs and discusses chronology; subject and structure coincide.

Having considered Dora's destination and her method of progress so thoroughly, we might well spend a moment considering her starting point, the occasion for her travel and development. Her journey begins as a response to the news of her father's death, and in the last scene Dora's private research is juxtaposed against his burial. The occasion is more than a circumstance, of course: Freud sees in it (if we may suspend our procedure for the sake of a comparison) one of the principal motives behind the dream: "Shall we be going astray if we suppose that the situation which formed the façade of the dream was a phantasy of revenge directed against her father? . . . According to the phantasy she had left home and gone among strangers, and her father's heart had broken with grief and with longing for her. Thus she would be revenged" (*Dora*, p. 98). Whether or not this reading, based on a large inference about Dora's motives for leaving home in the dream, is appropriate, the dream suggests an entirely different relationship between the two events, one which explains the connection between travelling and death throughout the dream, not just in the first section. We saw, in the travelling of the middle and last sections, a metaphor for the relationship between time and knowledge. We may also wonder whether Dora's original travelling, from her home to the strange town which begins the dream, is not also metaphorical. If it is, then the immediate background to the first scene in the dream consists of a passage of time rather than distance and has presumably led to a different state of knowledge, as represented by the dream's opening setting. It has also "led to" her father's death, at least chronologically. This would establish some connection between the fact of her father's death and the new state of knowledge—a connection which is clear in the final scene of the dream.

This new state of knowledge, Dora's starting point in the dream, might better be termed a state of ignorance: she left home "without her parents' knowledge." Specifically, Dora has broken the connection of knowledge or understanding with her father; after her move, neither knows anything about the other. Seen against this background, the father's death seems directly to extend the implications of Dora's travelling by severing the tie between father and daughter completely. Once the tie has been thus cut, Dora can begin her journey "home," in search of herself. Thus the dream describes a developmental sequence for Dora. She frees herself from the bond with her father by moving away; when that is accomplished and her father is "dead" to her, she "can" return home; the home she returns to is her private room and the big book, her research into herself. The death of her father upon which the dream is built is at least partly metaphorical.

The transition from self-imposed ignorance to private research is treated in the center section, of course, and there Dora's father is replaced by the mysterious man in the woods who appears exactly in the middle of the dream. This character is as paradoxical as anything else in the middle section. He is alive and present, in contrast to her father; he offers her his company, and she leaves him behind as she had her father. He offers information to Dora, but the information is problematical and discouraging, and we cannot tell whether it advances Dora's search in any way. It is not clear whether the entire encounter in the woods is a step in Dora's progress towards the station or whether it has been a diversion from which she must return in order to continue looking. Insofar as the man in the woods represents a substitute or successor to Dora's father, as well as an alternate, we may guess why his offer of help is refused. If Dora were to accept his company she would be simultaneously accepting her father through him and rejecting her father by accepting the man as his substitute. But Dora's goal is to be free of her father, not connected to him by any bond of either acceptance or rejection. She wishes to dissociate herself in order to begin her private research. The man who offers his help, therefore, represents an unacceptable option to her. In rejecting him here, Dora is dramatically reenacting the dynamic process which had led her to the first scene of the dream, the starting point of her independence.

We have reached a stopping point in our own journey; at least we have come as far as the limited vehicle of this analysis can bring us. Other details would prove repetitious on examination, and it is clear that a literary reading of Dora's dream will remain incomplete without a good deal of information about the personal meaning of the elements in the dream, the private language and symbolism of the individual psyche. But two other points are equally clear and of paramount importance for our project. First, Dora's dream includes a veritable wealth of features which psychoanalytic theory entirely overlooks. The dream is a busy complexity of plot, character, imagery, structure, theme, and tone. The mere fact that these elements exist in the dream at all requires a major adjustment in the Freudian description of dreams. The dream is full of riches that have gone unnoticed. How important these aesthetic features are, or how they may be related to the details of a psychoanalytic reading, are further questions, of course. But before we even begin to address those questions we must appreciate the significance of this very immediate fact.

The second point to be emphasized here is equally significant. Not only does the dream contain literary elements, it orders them. It is not a random sample of images and themes, characters and bits of plot. Rather, each element in the dream enjoys multiple relationships with others, and the dream as a whole coordinates its various elements impressively. We are dealing with a coherent artifact and, in some ways, a sophisticated one. The fact that this artifact is reluctant to yield up its meaning is no argument that it is not coherent. We are confronted, simply, with the product of an unknown culture, the culture of a private psyche, and our understanding of the coherence of its expression depends on our learning the terms and values of that culture. The dream is no rebus, as Freud would have us believe. It is not a jumble of unrelated fragments which can only be understood individually, only in terms of their origins, and which have no immediate relation to one another. The analysis we have just completed suggests a very different hypothesis: that the elements of the manifest dream not only relate to one another, but influence one another. That is, they mutually confer and modify meaning, and no one of them is completely understandable without reference to the others. Our analysis suggests an exact reversal of Freud's position: the dream cannot be fully understood if it is treated merely as a rebus.[19]

It is apparent, then, that a literary reading produces a result very different from Freud's. I am not referring to the fact that the literary reading is incomplete; we will later see that there are specific and definable reasons for its limits, and we will also see that Freud's psychoanalytic reading is equally incomplete. Our next step, therefore, is to measure the literary reading against Freud's and against the facts of the case history. Is there any relationship between the two interpretations, or are they unrelated alternatives, reflecting the interests of two different interpreters? Insofar as they are distinct, which tells us most about Dora's dream, and even about Dora?

Chapter Three

Freud on Dora's Dream

Dora

When the girl whom Freud calls Dora was brought to him for treatment on or before October 14, 1900, she was eighteen years old and came to him with a history of hysterical symptoms.[1] Since early childhood she had been especially attached to her father but had never gotten along with her mother. When she was six her family moved, for the sake of her father's health, to a town which Freud designates as "B——" and there they made the acquaintance of Herr and Frau K., beginning a complex involvement that had much to do with Dora's symptoms. Frau K. nursed Dora's father through his tuberculosis while Dora's mother avoided the sickroom. Dora, at seven, was troubled by bedwetting. When she was eight she developed a chronic dyspnoea.[2] When she was twelve her father visited Freud in Vienna to be treated for syphilis, and Dora experienced headaches and severe coughing fits accompanied by loss of voice. By this time the K.'s had become close intimates: Dora's father was clearly having a love affair with Frau K.; Herr K. paid particular attention to Dora, bestowing gifts and kindnesses upon her; and Dora spent considerable time with the couple, often looking after their small children.

When Dora was fourteen Herr K. kissed her and afterwards she avoided his company for a time, though she did not reveal the incident or attempt to break off relations entirely. In the summer of 1898, when Dora was sixteen, she and her father passed through Vienna on their way to join the K.'s at a lakeside resort. Dora's father introduced her to Freud. At the resort, Dora's father was to stay a few days in a hotel while Dora planned to spend several weeks living with the K.'s. While Dora was at the resort she learned from the K.'s governess that Herr K. had seduced her and then grown tired of her. Dora had noticed, when she arrived, that the governess and Herr K. scarcely spoke to each other. The governess explained to her in private that she was hoping for a change of heart on Herr K.'s part and a return of his affections; her parents had written to her to leave the house immediately or else she would not be permitted to return home.

On one particular outing during this stay, Herr K. and Dora took a boat trip across the lake and, after they had landed, he made a proposal to her, repeating some of the phrases that Dora knew he had used to seduce the governess. Dora slapped him in the face before he could finish and ran away, intending to walk home around the lake. When she met a man who told her that the walk would take two and a half hours, she returned to the boat and rode back with Herr K. That afternoon Dora woke from her nap to find Herr K. standing over her. She asked Frau K. for a key to the room and the next morning locked herself in while she was dressing. The key disappeared; Dora, convinced that Herr K. had removed it, determined to leave with her father, who had been meeting Frau K. early each morning.

Two weeks after Dora arrived home with her father, she reported the incident to her mother. Her father, on learning of it, wrote to Herr K. demanding an explanation. At a subsequent meeting Herr K. told him that the incident had not taken place, that Dora had imagined it, and that Dora had been spending her time reading "Mantegazza's *Physiology of Love* and books of that sort in their house on the lake" (*Dora*, p. 26).[3] Dora's father chose to believe Herr K. Two and a half years later he brought Dora to Freud for analysis; he wanted Freud to "try and bring her to reason" (*Dora*, p. 26).

Freud first mentions Dora in a letter to Fliess written on October 14, 1900: "It has been a lively time, and I have a new patient, a girl of eighteen; the case has opened smoothly to my collection of picklocks."[4] The analysis ended on December 31, 1900, when Dora announced to Freud without warning that they were conducting their last session. During that short time she reported two dreams, one of them a few weeks before the end of the analysis and the second dream, which we have been discussing, only a few hours before the end of the analysis. The first and shorter dream was one which Dora had had three nights in succession at the lake—the three nights between Herr K.'s removal of her key and her departure with her father—and it had recurred during the analysis:

> *A house was on fire. My father was standing beside my bed and woke me up. I dressed quickly. Mother wanted to stop and save her jewel-case; but Father said: "I refuse to let myself and my two children be burnt for the sake of your jewel-case." We hurried downstairs, and as soon as I was outside I woke up.* (*Dora*, p. 64)

Freud easily develops the associations he needs to construct his analysis of this short dream. On arriving at the resort lodgings, Dora's father had noticed that the small wooden house was without a lightning rod and had "openly said he was afraid of fire" (*Dora*, p. 65). Her father standing over her bed in the dream recalled not only Herr K. standing over her while she was napping on the afternoon of his proposition, but also a childhood scene in which her father stood over her to wake her in order to prevent her wetting her bed (*Dora*, pp. 66, 71–73). At the lakeside lodge, Dora dressed quickly because of her fear of Herr K. (*Dora*, p. 67). The jewel case, recalling gifts from Dora's father to her mother and another from Herr K. to Dora, represented the virginity which was in danger in Herr K.'s "burning" house (*Dora*, pp. 68–70).[5] Finally, Freud summarizes his reading:

> The dream from the analysis of which we have derived this information corresponded, as we have seen, to an intention which Dora carried with her into her sleep. It was therefore repeated each night until the intention had been carried out; and it reappeared years later when an occasion arose for form-

> ing an analogous intention. The intention might have been consciously expressed in some such words as these: "I must fly from this house, for I see that my virginity is threatened here; I shall go away with my father, and I shall take precautions not to be surprised while I am dressing in the morning." These thoughts were clearly expressed in the dream; they formed part of a mental current which had achieved consciousness and a dominating position in waking life. Behind them can be discerned obscure traces of a train of thought which formed part of a contrary current and had consequently been suppressed. This other train of thought culminated in the temptation to yield to the man. . . . (*Dora*, p. 85)

In identifying the infantile material, Freud clarifies the function of Dora's father in the dream and in the resort scenario, thus producing a most valuable insight:

> Why should a recollection have emerged of her bed-wetting when she was a child. . . . it was only by the help of this train of thought that it was possible to suppress the other thoughts which were so intensely occupied with the temptation to yield. . . . The child decided to fly *with* her father; in reality she fled *to* her father because she was afraid of the man who was pursuing her; she summoned up an infantile affection for her father so that it might protect her against her present affection for a stranger. (*Dora*, pp. 85–86)

Finally, Freud makes a beginning on a transference interpretation but, as Steven Marcus points out, does not develop it: "His extraordinary analysis of Dora's first dream is inadequate on just this count. He is only dimly and marginally aware of his central place in it (he is clearly incorporated into the figure of Dora's father), comments on it only as an addition to Dora's own addendum to the dream, and does nothing to exploit it."[6] Freud first raises the question of his role in the dream, however, in a footnote attached to a long paragraph concerned with Herr K., not Dora's father, in which he explains to Dora that she has *not* succeeded in putting that gentleman behind her: "I added: 'Moreover, the re-appearance of the dream in the last few days forces me to the conclusion that you consider that the same situation has arisen once again, and that you have decided to give up the treatment—to which, after all, it is only your father who makes you come.' The sequel showed how correct my guess had been" (*Dora*, p. 70, n. 2).[7] Freud's role in the dream is confirmed and further detailed in an addendum which Dora introduced the following day, but once again he sees that role only in terms of Herr K. rather than in terms of his connection with Dora's father:

> The interpretation of the dream now seemed to me to be complete. But Dora brought me an addendum to the dream on the very next day. She had forgotten to relate, she said, that each time after waking up she had smelt smoke. Smoke, of course, fitted in well with fire, but it also showed that the dream had a special relation to myself; for when she used to assert that there was nothing concealed behind this or that, I would often say by way of rejoinder: "There can be no smoke without fire!" Dora objected, however, to such a purely personal interpretation, saying that Herr K. and her father were passionate smokers—as I am too, for the matter of that. . . .
> . . . the addendum to the dream could scarcely mean anything else than the longing for a kiss, which, with a smoker, would necessarily smell of smoke. But a kiss had passed between Herr K. and Dora some two years further back. . . . Taking into consideration, finally, the indications which seemed to point to there having been a transference on to me—since I am a smoker too—I came to the conclusion that the idea had probably occurred to her one day during a session that she would like to have a kiss from me. This would have been the exciting cause which led her to repeat the warning dream and to form her intention of stopping the treatment.
>
> (*Dora*, pp. 73, 74)

Freud relates his transference reading to the suppressed "contrary current" of thought behind the dream, that is, to Dora's suppressed inclination to yield to Herr K. In so doing, Freud aligns himself with Herr K. rather than with Dora's father, who promises escape from the danger. Yet there is good reason, as we will see shortly in another connection, to consider the relationship between Freud and Dora's father in Dora's mind. Furthermore, Freud's choice of roles here creates certain difficulties in fitting the transference reading to the details of the dream because Dora's attitude towards and expectations of her father had altered dramatically since her dependence upon him more than two years earlier.[8] But this subject, too, can better be explored in connection with Dora's second dream, which treats these topics in much more detail.

From this brief summary of the background of the case, then, we can gather the skeleton of information we need to begin examining Freud's analysis of the second dream. That obviously more complicated production evokes a more complex—and more problematical—response from Freud. It will be clearest if we deal with the material in two stages. First, we can consider Freud's treatment of six major images of the dream (the strange town, the letter, the station, the temporal references, the thick woods, and the book); it is in connection with these major elements that Freud produces most of the associational and background material for his analysis, although he does not, of course, systematically relate these images to each other or attempt to discover a coherent pattern which would encompass them all. In the course of reviewing this material, we will find it necessary to consider a number of connections between the dream elements and Dora's personal history which Freud, for some reason, overlooks. Secondly, we can examine Freud's two summary statements of his conclusions about the dream, noting the contradiction between them and their uncertain relationship to some of the data of the case.

Dora's Images

Freud begins his work by finding associations for the opening scene of the dream, the unknown town where Dora finds herself walking about. Freud determines that the dream town is not B——, where Dora and her father first became involved with the K.'s, but he does not try to discover whether the scene bears any relation to the factory town where Dora lived for a year when she was about fourteen or, more importantly, to Vienna. Nor does he consider Dresden, which is connected with some parts of the dream by a certain chain of associations. The most literal source for the dream town, it seems, is an album of pictures from a German health resort, sent to Dora by a young engineer who probably "intended to come forward as a suitor one day"; Dora had looked at this album the day before the dream and "one of the pictures was of a square with a monument in it" (*Dora*, pp. 95–96). Freud also relates two visits to new towns: Dora had been showing a visiting cousin around Vienna the day before the dream, and this reminded her of her own earlier visit to Dresden where she had spent two hours in front of a Madonna in the gallery there (*Dora*, p. 96). Freud concludes, "But what was most evident was that in this first part of the dream she was identifying herself with a young man. This young man was wandering about in a strange place, he was striving to reach a goal, but he was being kept back, he needed patience and must wait. If in all this she had been thinking of the engineer, it would have been appropriate for the goal to have been the possession of a woman, of herself. But instead of this it was—a station" (*Dora*, pp. 96–97). The mention of the station leads Freud on to the second scene of the dream, and from there on to other topics, more or less directly pertinent to various details of the dream. He returns to this topic thirteen pages later in a footnote: "Finally, we can see the action of the fourth and most deeply buried group of thoughts—those relating to her love for Frau K.—in the fact that the phantasy of defloration is represented from the man's point of view (her identification of herself with her admirer who lived abroad) . . ." (*Dora*, pp. 110n–111n). At this point, Freud's line of thought is confusing. His conclusion is based on his own implicit condensation of two distinct images in the dream, the town at the beginning and the woods in the second scene.[9] He chooses to read Dora's tour of the unknown town as her adoption of a masculine sexual role, via an identification with the young engineer who sent her the pictures from which this dream town was constructed and who was himself, presumably, in a strange town.[10] But the "symbolic geography of sex" (more on this later) which the masculinized Dora must penetrate in order to create a fantasy of defloration is in the middle of the second scene; likewise, the several symbols for female genitals which Freud proposes are located in the second and third scenes of the dream. In order to unite these symbolic partners, therefore, we must either merge the two sceneries (ignoring the unmistakable structural division of the dream) or we must assume that Dora, having acquired a masculine role in the first scene, carries it with her into the second. There is a certain awkwardness in this last alternative, of course, since the masculine role derived, precisely, from the scene itself, from Dora's presence in the strange town. It is much easier, as we will see later, to assign Dora a feminine role in the second scene, and in fact this would better support Freud's interest in a fantasy of defloration related to Dora's love for Frau K. At this point, however, it is clear that we have long ago ceased to explicate the image of the town.

In Freud's interpretation of the first image, then, we are immediately led to associations that draw us away from the image rather than explaining it. What is the unknown town with its monument? Even if we accepted Freud's interpretation of it, his treatment of it as a clue leading away to a latent dream-thought, why has the dream-thought been referred to by this particular image? But it is hard to accept Freud's commentary as an interpretation of the image itself, even though he does produce pertinent background material. Freud does not help us understand how the image fits into its context in the dream or, what is more surprising, how it fits into the biographical context of Dora's life. His construction of a male role for Dora is based on the flimsiest materials: because she pictures herself in the same town a young man inhabits, she must be implying her desire to be male rather than, for example, her desire to be in the same town the young man inhabits. Finally, however, he leaves the image behind, without elucidating it, in favor of other interests.

Freud's brief treatment of the second major image, the letter announcing the death of Dora's father, creates difficulties of another sort. On the one hand, a valuable allusion is identified: in an addendum to the dream Dora specified that the contents of the letter included an idiosyncratic punctuation mark—"Now he is dead, and if you like? you can come." The odd punctuation reproduces a similar device in the letter from Frau K. that invited Dora to the lake resort where Herr K. made his proposal to her. Thus the letter Dora receives from her mother in the dream adopts Frau K.'s device and thereby recalls that most significant invitation. Freud does not pursue this point, but moves on to the scene at the lake and then to other matters. We may very well wonder why the dream has assigned Frau K.'s idiosyncrasy to Dora's mother and why the death of Dora's father has been thus associated with Dora's traumatic experience by the lake.

But most of Freud's commentary on the letter is connected with Dora's supposed motive of revenge:

> This brings us to the *contents of the letter* in the dream. Her father was dead, and she had left home by her own choice. In connection with this letter I at once reminded Dora of the farewell letter which she had written to her parents or had at least composed for their benefit (p. 23). This letter had been intended to give her father a fright, so that he should give up Frau K.; or at any rate to take revenge on him if he could not be induced to do that. We are here concerned with the subject of her death and of her father's death.... According to the phantasy she had left home and gone among strangers, and her father's heart had broken with grief and with longing for her. Thus she would be revenged. (*Dora*, pp. 97–98)

The letter Freud refers to was written not long before Dora began her treatment and was one of the factors, apparently, which figured in the decision to bring her to Freud:

> One day her parents were thrown into a state of great alarm by finding on the girl's writing-desk, or inside it, a letter in which she took leave of them because, as she said, she could no longer endure her life.
>
> This affair of the letter came up in the course of one of our sessions (p. 97f.), and the girl showed signs of astonishment. "How on earth," she asked, "did they find the letter? It was shut up in my desk." But since she knew that her parents had read this draft of a farewell letter, I conclude that she had herself arranged for it to fall into their hands.
>
> (*Dora*, p. 23 and n. 1)

Assuming that the motive for Dora's real letter was revenge and assuming that the real letter and the dream letter, in spite of their obvious differences, have equivalent implications, we are still faced with several unexplained features of the dream letter. Presumably, Freud would paraphrase its contents ("She wrote saying that as I had left home without my parents' knowledge she had not wished to write to me to say that Father was ill. 'Now he is dead, and if you like? you can come.'") with something like this: "Now that your father is dead, your revenge is accomplished, and you need not stay away any longer." This leaves unexplained, however, the fact that the letter comes from Dora's mother (in order to pinpoint the target of Dora's revenge by excluding her mother?) and the fact that the letter includes an allusion to Frau K.'s invitation (in order to reveal the motive for Dora's revenge on her father?). More importantly, why did Dora's mother not wish to write earlier "*because*," as the dream says, Dora had left home "without her parents' knowledge"? And since there is a question as to whether Dora's real letter was or was not intended for her parents' knowledge, might not the dream letter cast some light on its real predecessor? The real letter was kept in Dora's writing desk, we are told, and we cannot help but wonder at a possible connection between that writing desk and the one at the end of the dream. Indeed, what connections exist between the dream letter and the dream desk?

In fact, however, Freud's imputation of a motive of revenge is based on insufficiently explored associations (between the dream letter and the real letter) and does not go very far in explaining the function of the letter within the dream. We cannot claim to understand the letter fully, for example, until we know what Dora returns home to, at its instigation. Nor should we overlook the ironic connections between the letter in scene one and the book on the writing desk in scene three.

In dealing with the next image, the station, Freud also simplifies its implications, though this time the intermediate materials, the associations, are more complex. The pivotal image of the station suggests only one thing to Freud: "The use of '*Bahnhof*' ['station'; literally, 'railway-court'] and '*Friedhof*' ['cemetery'; literally, 'peace-court'] to represent the female genitals was striking enough in itself, but it also served to direct my awakened curiosity to the similarly formed '*Vorhof*' ['vestibulus'; literally, 'fore-court']—an anatomical term for a particular region of the female genitals" (*Dora*, p. 99). Freud supplements this observation with a footnote: "Moreover, a 'station' is used for purposes of '*Verkehr*' ['traffic,' 'intercourse,' 'sexual intercourse']: this fact determines the psychical coating in a number of cases of railway phobia" (*Dora*, p. 99, n. 2).[11] Freud connects the sexual significance of the station to that of the thick wood which he has related to the actual scene by the lake as well as to the scenery of a painting Dora had recently viewed: "Yes. The *wood* in the dream had been just like the wood by the shore of the lake, the wood in which the scene she had just described once more had taken place. But she had seen precisely the same thick wood the day before, in a picture at the Secessionist exhibition. In the background of the picture there were *nymphs*" (*Dora*, p. 99). Altogether, then, the sexual imagery reads as follows:

> The phantasy of defloration formed the second component of the situation. The emphasis upon the difficulty of getting forward and the anxiety felt in the dream indicated the stress which the dreamer was so ready to lay upon her virginity—a point alluded to in another place by means of the Sistine Madonna. These sexual thoughts gave an unconscious ground-colouring to the wishes (which were perhaps merely kept secret) concerned with the suitor who was waiting for her in Germany. We have already recognized the phantasy of revenge as the first component of the same situation in the dream. The two components do not coincide completely, but only in part.
> (*Dora*, p. 100, n. 1)

In order to arrive at this construction, Freud has, this time, made elaborate links among manifest elements. The station is interpreted sexually and is related to the cemetery, which is interpreted sexually, as well as to the thick woods, also interpreted sexually. These images have been further related to the opening scene, the strange town. That image was based on the album of pictures sent Dora by her potential suitor; before looking at the pictures the day before the dream, Dora had asked her mother, "Where is the box?" (in which the album was kept). Freud links this question to the dream question, "Where is the station?" (*Dora*, pp. 95–97). Since, naturally, the box must be read sexually, the town which the dream constructed from the pictures contained in the box can be linked, via the question, directly to the sexual railway station. Freud summarizes these trains of thought with the comment, "Here was a symbolic geography of sex! . . . If this interpretation were correct, therefore, there lay concealed behind the first situation in the dream a phantasy of defloration, the phantasy of a man seeking to force an entrance into the female genitals" (*Dora*, pp. 99–100).

Freud's interpretation here violates the order of the manifest dream. He has connected the town, the station, the woods, and the cemetery in his "symbolic geography of sex." In the dream, however, these images are distributed among three separate geographies, and, as we have seen, the network of parallels and contrasts that unites these three scenes depends upon their being treated distinctly. There is, of course, the verbal echo *Bahnhof-Friedhof*, which is a significant clue. But the station and the cemetery are not *equivalent* images merely because they are *related* images. The function of the verbal echo is to link them causally, thematically, and ironically.

Freud's reading of a phantasy of defloration is safely vague, in spite of the intricacy of some of the associations which led to it.[12] It is, I think, not entirely clear who is deflowering whom, at least at every point in this chain of images, nor are the distinct features of the separate images taken into account, nor is their particular sequence considered.[13] What can it mean, for example, that Dora penetrates the thick wood effortlessly but is paralyzed by sexual anxiety in front of the station?[14] If both wood and station are symbols for the female genitals, why is the symbolic sexual experience repeated, and why is it varied? What should we make of the fact that Dora seeks out one of these symbols, the station, but avoids another, the cemetery? In sum, it may well be that Dora experienced a fantasy of defloration, in either a masculine or a feminine role, but that fantasy has not been convincingly coordinated with the details of the dream, nor does it seem to offer major insight into the workings of the dream.

It is in the middle of this "sexual geography" that the next element appears, the odd temporal references. The first of them, the answer of "five minutes" which Dora receives when she asks directions to the station, produces a day residue:

> *She asked quite a hundred times.* . . . This led to another exciting cause of the dream, and this time to one that was less indifferent. On the previous evening they had had company, and afterwards her father had asked her to fetch him the brandy: he could not get to sleep unless he had taken some brandy. She had asked her mother for the key of the sideboard; but the latter had been deep in conversation, and had not answered

her, until Dora had exclaimed with the exaggeration of impatience: "I've asked you *a hundred times* already where the key is." As a matter of fact, she had of course only repeated the question about *five times*. (*Dora*, p. 97)

This, of course, leads to still another sexual reference, one which is not explicit in the dream: "'Where is the *key*?' seems to me to be the masculine counterpart to the question 'Where is the *box*?' They are therefore questions referring to—the genitals" (*Dora*, p. 97). In this reading, therefore, Freud discounts the term "five minutes" in itself; it is only important insofar as it leads to another detail, the image of the key, for which it stands in the dream. There is, however, a connection between the phrase and Dora's experience which Freud has overlooked. It is the middle section of the dream which most specifically recalls the temptation scene by the lake. That middle scene divides into three subsections: 1) Dora asks for directions to the station and is told "five minutes" about a hundred times; 2) Dora enters the thick wood where a man tells her "two and a half hours more"; and 3) Dora sees the station but cannot reach it. The reply of "five minutes" is the main substance of the first of these three subsections. If we compare the entire middle scene of the dream to the actual events by the lake, this subsection corresponds, in position, to Herr K.'s proposal, after which Dora actually did go into a thick wood, meet a man, and so on. But what relation is there between looking for the station and the repeated answer of "five minutes," on the one hand, and Herr K.'s proposal on the other? Neither of the two accounts of that scene in the case history offers the slightest clue (*Dora*, pp. 25–26, 98–99). But the figure five does appear prominently in connection with that experience; in discussing Dora's first dream, Freud asked her,

"Did you have the dream during your first nights at L—— or during your last ones? in other words, before or after the scene in the wood by the lake of which we have heard so much?" . . .
Her first reply was that she did not know, but after a while she added: "Yes. I think it was after the scene."

So now I knew that the dream was a reaction to that experience. But why had it recurred there three times? I continued with my questions: "How long did you stop on at L——after the scene?"

"Four days more. On the fifth day I went away with Father."

(*Dora*, pp. 65–66) [15]

The entire five-day period was a time of anxiety for Dora. After coming back from the scene of the proposal, she woke from her nap that afternoon to find Herr K. standing over her. She obtained a key from Frau K. and on the second morning locked herself in the bedroom while she was dressing. That same afternoon the key disappeared, and on that night (the second after the proposition) Dora first had the dream which signalled her resolution to escape from the situation. The dream recurred on the third and fourth nights after the proposition; on the fifth day Dora made her father take her home (*Dora*, pp. 66–67).

The five-day period of stress and anxiety would certainly be an experience worth referring to in the second dream, as well as the first; and it is obviously pertinent to the topic of the middle scene, especially since it was during this five-day period that Dora made the decision to escape from Herr K. altogether. But if the "five minutes" of the dream refers to the five days of Dora's experience, then there is some difficulty in the chronology of the dream for the five days began with the scene in the woods and continued after it, whereas in the dream the phrase "five minutes" occurs before the scene in the woods. It is tempting to claim yet another example of the dream's bent for paradox here, but that is not necessary. It is true that the two chronologies do not coincide; the dissonance does not mean, however, that they are not related. Rather, this section of the dream is trying to reproduce two different real chronologies at once, and since that is not possible, it must resort to the strategem of Shakespeare's *Othello* in merely suggesting each of the two chronologies, conflicting though they may be. They do *not* conflict thematically, and that is precisely why the dream has gone to the trouble of juggling them. The first of the two real chronologies is the literal sequence of the events at the lake:

1. Herr K. makes his proposal to Dora;
2. A man in the woods says "two and a half hours more" to Dora;
3. Dora finds her escape (her "station"), but cannot reach it (because it is too far away).

In this sequence, the escape she sought in the woods may be compared to the station she seeks in her dream woods, and the actual scene of Herr K.'s proposition, therefore, is only represented in the dream by Dora's reaction to it, by her quest for an escape. "Where is the station?" in the dream matches "Where is my escape?" in the real scene. This corresponds to Dora's actual response to Herr K.: she interrupted him and "hurried away" (*Dora*, p. 98). Later, Dora met the man in the woods and, later still, she found a "station," an escape, and left the resort with her father. As far as this goes, the dream chronology corresponds with the real chronology of the event.

But the dream is retrospective and, since it is looking back on the past, it knows the outcome of the events that it refers to. It can, therefore, present an earlier event in the light of a later development. This is what happens when the phrase "five minutes" is interpolated into the chronology just sketched out. When Dora asks, "Where is my escape?" she receives a double answer which actually reproduces her experience at the lake more fully. Most immediately, her escape was to run away from Herr K. and the actual spot of the proposal. In this sense her release was only "minutes" away, and Dora hurried into the thick wood. As it turned out, however, that first escape was a very temporary one, and Dora was not completely freed from the danger of Herr K.'s attention until four days later when she left with her father. The dream, by conflating the two chronologies (that of the single afternoon and that of the whole five-day period), answers the question twice and relates the two answers to one another as well. (We will see later on that this sort of double chronology, once started, continues to function significantly in the dream.) Thus the phrase "five minutes" can be related to Dora's experience, and the significance it thus acquires, carried back into its context in the dream, clarifies its relationship to other immediate details.

The second temporal reference in the dream produces much richer associations. This phrase, "two and a half hours more," recalls the literal events of the lakeside scene:

> No sooner had she grasped the purport of his words than she had slapped him in the face and hurried away. . . . In order to avoid meeting him again she had wanted to get back to L—— on foot, by walking round the lake, and *she had asked a man whom she met how far it was*. On his replying that it was "*Two and a half hours*," she had given up her intention and had after all gone back to the boat, which left soon afterwards. . . . Yes. The *wood* in the dream had been just like the wood by the shore of the lake, the wood in which the scene she had just described once more had taken place. (*Dora*, pp. 98–99)

In retelling the dream (Freud does not mention exactly when this occurred) Dora amended the reference to "two hours," and this is the figure Freud pursues in the associations. Freud recounts Dora's visit to Dresden:[16]

> On that occasion she had been a stranger and had wandered about, not failing, of course, to visit the famous picture gallery. Another (male) cousin of hers, who was with them and knew Dresden, had wanted to act as a guide and take her round the gallery. *But she declined and went alone*, and stopped in front of the pictures that appealed to her. She remained *two hours* in front of the Sistine Madonna, rapt in silent admiration. When I asked her what had pleased her so much about the picture she could find no clear answer to make. At last she said: "The Madonna." (*Dora*, p. 96)

Further material comes to light when Dora announces, at the beginning of the third hour spent interpreting the dream, that it is to be her last hour. Freud asks her when she decided to end the analysis and Dora replies, "A fortnight ago, I think." Freud reacts, "That sounds just like a maidservant or a governess—a fortnight's warning," and this leads to further information (*Dora*, p. 105). At the lake resort Dora had discovered that the governess who was employed by the K.'s to help with the two children (Dora had frequently played this role in an informal way) had been seduced by Herr K. and subsequently had been rejected by him. The girl had not yet given her notice (two weeks, normally), although her parents had written her that she must. In Dora's words:

> "Well, there was a young girl in the house, who was the children's governess; and she behaved in the most extraordinary way to Herr K. She never said good morning to him, never answered his remarks, never handed him anything at table when he asked for it, and in short treated him like thin air. For that matter he was hardly any politer to her. A day or two before the scene by the lake, the girl took me aside and said she had something to tell me. She then told me that Herr K. had made advances to her at a time when his wife was away for several weeks; he had made violent love to her and had implored her to yield to his entreaties, saying that he got nothing from his wife, and so on." — "Why, those are the very words he used afterwards, when he made his proposal to you and you gave him the slap in his face" (p. 98). — "Yes. She had given way to him, but after a little while he had ceased to care for her, and since then she hated him." — "And this governess had given warning?" — "No. She meant to give warning. She told me that as soon as she felt she was thrown over she had told her parents what had happened. They were respectable people living in Germany somewhere. Her parents said that she must leave the house instantly: and, as she failed to do so, they wrote to her saying that they would have nothing more to do with her, and that she was never to come home again." — "And why had she not gone away?" — "She said she meant to

wait a little longer, to see if there might not be some change in Herr K. She could not bear living like that any more, she said, and if she saw no change she should give warning and go away." — "And what became of the girl?" — "I only know that she went away." — "And she did not have a child as a result of the adventure?" — "No."   (*Dora*, pp. 105–106)

When Herr K. made his proposal to Dora, he spoke the same phrase to her that he had used in seducing the young governess, and Dora waited exactly two weeks after the incident before reporting it to her mother. It would seem that the period of "two hours" in the dream makes important references to these three instances of giving notice: that of the K.'s governess after her seduction and disappointment, that of Dora in telling her mother, and that of Dora in deciding to end her analysis. In this last case the parallel is closest; not only did Dora decide to end the analysis two weeks in advance, but the dream which makes use of these very references was presented to Freud a little more than two hours before the end.[17]

These associations do not, however, exhaust the possibilities. Dora's history, as it emerges in the case study, seems almost organized into pairs of events. Most prominently, Herr K. made advances to Dora on two occasions (the kiss when she was fourteen and the proposal by the lake when she was sixteen); furthermore, the proposal by the lake was the second maneuver of that particular kind he had made (the first involving the young governess). In a sense, Dora, who had long been devoted to the K.'s children and who had spent much time caring for them, was being put in the position of being the second "governess" to be seduced and perhaps later rejected by Herr K. Even Freud recognizes that this realization was an important factor in Dora's refusal of Herr K. (*Dora*, pp. 106–107), although he seriously underestimates its importance. Again, Dora decided on the second day of her five-day ordeal at L——to leave with her father and remove herself from Herr K.'s influence. Dora was also seeing Freud for the second time: she had met him two years before, on her way with her father to L—— and the seduction scene by the lake. At that earlier meeting Freud had suggested therapy. It is curious, in fact, that most of the important events in Dora's history, as Freud presents it, arrange themselves in two-year intervals; perhaps that period of time had acquired some rhythmic or symbolic significance for Dora.[18]

It is clear, therefore, that the reference to "two hours" in the dream is a seminal allusion to a number of Dora's circumstances. Freud recognizes each of several allusions individually but stops short of coordinating them. That last step is not difficult, however. That time period, in every case, was the time required to escape from scenes of temptation and conflict which Dora experienced both literally and symbolically.[19] In the actual scene by the lake, two and a half hours was the time it would have taken Dora to walk back to L—— alone, that is, to walk away from Herr K.'s insulting proposal. With regard to the K.'s governess, two weeks was the notice which she should have given Herr K. (and eventually did) in order to escape from her difficult situation. After Herr K.'s proposal, Dora waited two weeks before telling her mother; that revelation, no doubt, was intended to resolve the conflict even more finally than her flight from the vicinity.[20] And the two weeks' "notice" to Freud, which she kept to herself, was the time required to free her from the situation of the analysis. This last fact suggests a parallel, of course; Dora must have viewed the analysis as a situation of temptation or conflict, though we cannot yet specify why. It may be that she simply wanted to escape from Freud's reconstruction—increasingly detailed and pertinent—of the painful experience with Herr K. But the timing of the analysis suggests otherwise: it was only in the last session, but it *was* in the last session, that Dora revealed the key to her experience, the essential information about the seduced governess. It is as if she had "decided" to communicate to Freud what he had not yet been able to discover for himself—or what she had been unwilling to reveal to him previously. But since she did communicate these details to him, in however indirect and belated a manner, was it a fear of discovery or of Freud's resurrecting the complete traumatic experience which moved her to end the analysis? Either is possible, of course, and, in a sense, her decision to break with Freud might have given her the license she needed to deliver the key information to him, to leave a parting note, perhaps, or a secret he had not been able to discover on his own. But however this sort of thinking may have played a part in Dora's decision, it will soon become apparent that there were other, more obvious reasons for her action.

Before moving to the last of the major images for which Freud obtained associations from Dora, we must pause a moment over a final peculiarity of this chronological reference. We have already noted that Dora, in retelling the dream to Freud, changed the phrase from "two and a half hours more" to "two hours [more?]." Freud misses the opportunity to comment on this revision even though, as he so clearly insisted elsewhere, the alteration ought to signal the repression of an important latent element, the revised version concealing the significance of the original manifestation. To Freud's keen eye, such secondary revisions served merely to expose the significance of the original element, thus alerting him to examine it all the more carefully.[21] But in this example the substitution accomplishes just the opposite effect; as Freud's own analysis proves, the figure "two" alludes much more precisely and immediately to the crux of the seduction scene and even goes a step further in suggesting the parallel between that experience and the analytic situation. The only "disguise" involved in this example is the blurring of one *literal* feature of the lakeside scene, the exact phrase "two and a half hours more" which was incorporated directly into the dream. But the allusion to the lakeside scene is not at all blurred; on the contrary, the figure "two" leads just as surely to it and in a way which is much more illuminating since it refers to the governess's talk with Dora (among other things) and thereby helps to shed light on Dora's reactions and motives during that crucial episode. And the dream scene itself retains more than enough hint of the lakeside scene that it recalls, in the images of the thick woods and the character of the man who appears there. In other words, the altered detail is very far from being a disguise of anything. It is an improved allusion which introduces several distinct factors and suggests parallels among them. In this case the merely literal detail has been replaced by a complex symbolic detail.

The last of the major images which Freud treats is the big book which Dora is reading in the last scene. The image, forgotten in Dora's first account of the dream, was added by her sometime during the first or second hour spent on the interpretation, and Freud takes this fact as a sign of the importance of the image: "I can quote this dream as fresh evidence for the correctness of an assertion made in my *Interpretation of Dreams* (Chapter VII, Section A; Standard Ed., 5, 518) to the effect that those pieces of a dream which are at first forgotten and are only subsequently remembered are invariably the most important from the point of view of understanding the dream" (*Dora*, p. 100, n. 2). But when Freud begins to examine the pertinent associations, he is quickly led away from the image of the book to the image of Dora walking up the stairs to her room in order to read the book—an image which appeared as the last of Dora's addenda to the dream. The two images share important connections, but Freud fails to exhaust the relevant material for either of them.

Freud relates the big book itself to two different events, one literal and one hypothetical. He begins by addressing the book's size:

> The emphasis here was upon the two details "calmly" and "big" in connection with "book." I asked whether the book was in encyclopaedia *format*, and she said it was. Now children never read about forbidden subjects in an encyclopaedia *calmly*. . . .
>
> At first she would not remember ever having read anything in an encyclopaedia; but she then admitted that a recollection of an occasion of the kind did occur to her, though it was of an innocent enough nature. At the time when the aunt she was so fond of had been so seriously ill and it had already been settled that Dora was to go to Vienna, a *letter* had come from another uncle, to say that they could not go to Vienna, as a

boy of his, a cousin of Dora's therefore, had fallen dangerously ill with appendicitis. Dora had thereupon looked up in the encyclopaedia to see what the symptoms of appendicitis were. From what she had then read she still recollected the characteristic localization of the abdominal pain. (*Dora*, pp. 100–101)

Thus, the literal event which Dora recalls was the occasion on which she consulted an encyclopedia for medical information. This leads Freud to consider Dora's hysterical attack of appendicitis nine months after the scene at the lake and her most unusual symptom of dragging her foot (*Dora*, pp. 101–104). The last symptom obviously relates to the image of Dora walking up the stairs so clearly in the dream. The big book, then, as a reference to Dora's medical research and thus to her appendicitis, leads to very promising connections. But what of the big book as a source of information on "forbidden subjects?" Freud continues:

Dora had therefore given herself an illness which she had read up about in the encyclopaedia, and she had punished herself for dipping into its pages. But she was forced to recognize that the punishment could not possibly apply to her reading the innocent article in question. It must have been inflicted as the result of a process of displacement, after another occasion of more guilty reading had become associated with this one; and the guilty occasion must lie concealed in her memory behind the contemporaneous innocent one.   (*Dora*, p. 102)

Freud thus proposes that Dora's medical research in the encyclopedia functions as a screen for her sexual research, but he does not uncover any memory or evidence for that sexual research; instead, he assumes the reality of this event.[22] It may well be that Dora, at some point in her life, consulted an encyclopedia out of sexual curiosity; there are, however, three other references for the dream image which are much nearer at hand. In the first place, Dora's current activities provide one likely significance for the big book in the dream: "She tried to avoid social intercourse, and employed herself—so far as she was allowed to by the fatigue and lack of concentration of which she complained—with attending lectures for women and with carrying on more or less serious studies" (*Dora*, p. 23). If this pattern is part of Dora's reaction to the traumatic scene at the lake and to its aftermath, then the parallel to the sequence in the dream is quite close. In the dream, Dora follows the section that refers to the lakeside scene, the middle section, with the reading of the big book: not only is she alone but, reading from her writing table (instead of writing), she is clearly avoiding social intercourse.

The big book, then, relates directly to Dora's experience at the lake by suggesting one of her reactions to that experience. It does so in a second, more emphatic way. Freud need not have postulated sexual researches in an encyclopedia, for Dora had done that work in another book, the *Physiology of Love* by Mantegazza, the book from which, according to Herr K., Dora constructed a fantasy of seduction. But this reference involves a good deal more than the guilty reading of forbidden subjects which Freud was looking for:

> Herr K. had been called to account by her father and uncle on the next occasion of their meeting, but he had denied in the most emphatic terms having on his side made any advances which could have been open to such a construction. He had then proceeded to throw suspicion upon the girl, saying that he had heard from Frau K. that she took no interest in anything but sexual matters, and that she used to read Mantegazza's *Physiology of Love* and books of that sort in their house on the lake. It was most likely, he had added, that she had been over-excited by such reading and had merely "fancied" the whole scene she had described.   (*Dora*, pp. 25–26)

In returning to this subject later, in another connection, Freud introduces more information and another, important complication:

> Indeed, I can say in general that I never heard her speak a harsh or angry word against the lady [Frau K.], although from the point of view of her supervalent thought she should have

regarded her as the prime author of her misfortunes. . . . For how had this woman to whom Dora was so enthusiastically devoted behaved to her? After Dora had brought forward her accusation against Herr K., and her father had written to him and had asked for an explanation, Herr K. had replied in the first instance by protesting sentiments of the highest esteem for her and by proposing that he should come to the manufacturing town to clear up every misunderstanding. A few weeks later, when her father spoke to him at B——, there was no longer any question of esteem. On the contrary, Herr K. spoke of her with disparagement, and produced as his trump card the reflection that no girl who read such books and was interested in such things could have any title to a man's respect. Frau K., therefore, had betrayed her and had calumniated her; for it had only been with her that she had read Mantegazza and discussed forbidden topics. It was a repetition of what had happened with [Dora's earlier] governess: Frau K. had not loved her for her own sake but on account of her father. Frau K. had sacrificed her without a moment's hesitation so that her relations with her father might not be disturbed. This mortification touched her, perhaps, more nearly and had a greater pathogenic effect than the other one, which she tried to use as a screen for it,—the fact that she had been sacrificed by her father. (*Dora*, p. 62)

Dora's book is very large indeed. In the final scene of the dream we see her reading it, not at the lake with Frau K., but alone, in the privacy of her room. The book is pivotal: it contains the sexual material that was the subject of Dora's traumatic experience; it alludes to the friendship and love Dora felt for Frau K., and therefore to Frau K.'s shocking betrayal of her; it makes reference to the aftermath of the lakeside scene, that is, to Dora's being accused of the very fault she had resisted; it puts Dora into the past, at a time when she was reading about such matters rather than dealing with them in actuality; it recalls, as Freud notes, the disturbing parallel between Frau

K.'s betrayal of Dora and an earlier governess's betrayal of her (and both for the same motive, interest in her father); it refers, by means of that parallel, to Dora's treatment by her father (who betrayed her in "handing her over" to Herr K. and betrayed her again by accepting Herr K.'s accusation against her) as well as to the disturbing parallel between Dora and the governess Herr K. had seduced and then cast aside; and it alludes, finally, to Dora's main current interest, her studies, a safer category of reading and a more solitary one than her reading in Mantegazza turned out to be.[23] There is no need to speculate about Dora's childhood sexual inquiries in an encyclopedia.[24]

In the final scene of the dream, we have already noted, Dora sees herself very clearly walking up the stairs to her room and the big book. Freud produces the pertinent biographical background for this image by revealing one of Dora's earlier hysterical symptoms, her dragging of her foot. This symptom was connected, most surprisingly from a physiological point of view, with Dora's "appendicitis," which occurred nine months after the lakeside scene. Freud reads that attack as a symbolic pregnancy and construes the lame foot as a metaphor ("she had made a 'false step'") that can be related to an actual injury to Dora's foot—"Yes, said Dora, once when she was a child she had twisted the same foot; she had slipped on one of the steps as she was going *downstairs*. . . . This had been a short time before the attack of nervous asthma in her eighth year" (*Dora*, p. 103). The lame foot, then, is to be associated with Dora's hysterical love for her father and, more immediately, with her imaginary "false step" at the lake. But she did *not* commit a false step at the lake—she did not succumb to Herr K.'s proposal—and in the dream her father is dead. The dream image of walking up the stairs is not merely a reference to these earlier situations, but an emphatic reversal of them. The dream "cures" Dora of her neurotic love for her father and for Herr K.[25]

A further reference, overlooked by Freud, adds an ironic dimension to the image. Dora was not the only one who suffered from an hysterical limp:

When they had returned to B——, her father had visited Frau K. every day at definite hours, while her husband was at his business. Everybody had talked about it. . . . When they had all gone for walks together, her father and Frau K. had always known how to manage things so as to be alone with each other. There could be no doubt that she had taken money from him. . . . And, while previously Frau K. had been an invalid and had even been obliged to spend months in a sanatorium for nervous disorders *because she had been unable to walk*, she had now become a healthy and lively woman.

(*Dora*, p. 33, emphasis added)

Nor has Freud ignored the parallel between Frau K.'s bad health and some of Dora's other symptoms: "But she had also learned from observing Frau K. what useful things illnesses could become. Herr K. spent part of the year in travelling. Whenever he came back, he used to find his wife in bad health, although, as Dora knew, she had been quite well only the day before. . . . [Dora's] illness was therefore a demonstration of her love for K., just as his wife's was a demonstration of her *dislike*. It was only necessary to suppose that her behaviour had been the opposite of Frau K.'s and that she had been ill when he was absent and well when he had come back" (*Dora*, pp. 38–39). The limp which Dora acquired began, we said, nine months after the scene at the lake, in conjunction with her "appendicitis" or, as Freud reads it, her false pregnancy. It would seem appropriate, therefore, to consider Dora's self-conscious walking up the stairs in the dream as a reference to Frau K. as well as to Herr K. Frau K.'s symptoms were cured by her love affair with Dora's father; Dora's limp is cured, in the dream, once her father is dead and her healthy walk leads her away from the lakeside scene and towards the private study of her big book.

When these reflections are linked to the big book and its associations and to Dora's current strategy in real life of replacing social intercourse with her studies, it is clear that the final scene suggests, in all its features, both a repudiation and a regression. The big book is meant to contrast with, not imitate, Mantegazza's *Physiology of Love*; Dora walks strongly upstairs without the incentive of a waiting lover; Dora reads in private, not with Frau K.[26] The final scene presents Dora in a pose of solitary independence. She has separated and distinguished herself from her father and from Frau K. as well as from Herr K.

In the case of these elements of the manifest dream we have been considering, Freud's analysis suffers from two limitations. Most obviously, he too often fails to adduce all the pertinent biographical material when he gathers associations for one of the images. No doubt part of the reason for this lies in the volume and complexity of the material, and surely the case history in its present state represents an enormous effort to select and organize. But, as we have seen, the additional connections are not superfluous ones, and in several instances they support a reading of the dream that is entirely different from Freud's. Since these additional connections are important, it is surprising that Freud has supplied them to us without using them himself.

Freud's second limitation is to be expected: he consistently refuses to acknowledge connections between one dream element and another, as his theory of dream construction obliges him to do. This means, first of all, that he must deal with each element in relative isolation, out of its context, notwithstanding the contextual support of the associations.[27] The effects of this limitation become apparent in some of Freud's more awkward readings (e.g., Dora's identification with the young engineer) but are even more noticeable in the numerous instances in which Freud leaves a topic unfinished or only superficially analyzed so that he can move on to another one. To a certain extent, the rich associations which a given image provokes distract him from the image itself, and he is all too willing to leave the manifest element behind in order to pursue the train of associations. The therapeutic value of this strategy is not, of course, our concern. Rather, we note that the strategy constantly detracts from the subject on which *we* are focussing, the characteristics of the dream itself.

Now, having treated important individual elements in the dream, and having gathered the most pertinent specifics from Dora's background and biography and from Freud's observations and interpretations, we are ready to complete our review of Freud's treatment by considering his summary statements on the dream.

Freud's Interpretations

Freud's examination of Dora's second dream occupied the final sessions of the analysis, and his investigation of the dream was truncated by Dora's sudden termination. Freud acknowledges the limitations imposed upon him by this circumstance; here the fragmentary nature of the case history is most apparent—a fact that, in turn, implies the dream's significance in the case since it refers to the analysis and its termination. After first quoting the dream Freud remarks: "It was not without some difficulty that the interpretation of this dream proceeded. In consequence of the peculiar circumstances in which the analysis was broken off—circumstances connected with the content of the dream—the whole of it was not cleared up. And for this reason, too, I am not equally certain at every point of the order in which my conclusions were reached. . . . I shall present the material produced during the analysis of this dream in the somewhat haphazard order in which it recurs to my mind" (*Dora*, p. 95).[28] At the end of this discussion he further remarks in a footnote, "It is not possible to understand it [the dream] thoroughly enough to allow of a synthesis being attempted" (*Dora*, p. 110n).[29] Notwithstanding these careful reservations, Freud sketches, in the same footnote, four important topics in the latent dream thoughts and hints at a fifth:

> A prominent piece of the dream is to be seen in the phantasy of revenge against her father, which stands out like a façade in

front of the rest. . . . Behind this phantasy lie concealed her thoughts of revenge against Herr K., for which she found an outlet in her behaviour to me. . . . Screened by these thoughts of revenge, glimpses can be caught in other places of material derived from tender phantasies based upon the love for Herr K. which still persisted unconsciously in Dora. . . . Finally, we can see the action of the fourth and most deeply buried group of thoughts—those relating to her love for Frau K. . . . Cruel and sadistic tendencies find satisfaction in this dream.

The fifth motif is hinted at elsewhere and eventually helps explain why Freud has placed his most comprehensive formulation of the dream's interpretation in a footnote. In the prefatory comment just quoted Freud ascribes some of the difficulties of interpreting this dream to "the peculiar circumstances in which the analysis was broken off—*circumstances connected with the content of the dream*" (emphasis added). That the dream refers to Freud and the analytic situation becomes apparent in several parallels and associations: two of the four motifs Freud proposes involve revenge, on Dora's father and on Herr K. respectively, and Freud describes Dora's termination of the analysis as an act of revenge against him: "I knew Dora would not come back again. Her breaking off so unexpectedly, just when my hopes of a successful termination of the treatment were at their highest, and her thus bringing those hopes to nothing—this was an unmistakable act of vengeance on her part" (*Dora*, p. 109). Furthermore, Freud's connection with Dora's father, which we discussed in relation to the first dream, is a renewed and strengthened possibility in the second dream which functions as a kind of terminal dream in the analysis. In effect, it tells Freud that the analysis is over by presenting the death of Dora's father.

Clearly, then, the second dream refers significantly to the analysis and its termination. It is odd that although Freud recognizes and describes a hidden role for himself in the first dream, he does not do so in the second. This time he makes no reference to any possible connection between himself and Dora's father until the postscript to the case history and, in fact, fails to exhaust the implications of a connection between Dora's father and Herr K. The omission is all the more noticeable because the dream is longer, more detailed, and more current than the first dream (in the sense that it is a new dream rather than the reappearance of an old one) and because the dream includes unmistakable and separate references to both men. In the next chapter we will be able to shed some light on this matter by considering the transference meaning of the dream in terms of our literary reading of the manifest text.

In the footnote summary itself we encounter difficulties of two quite different sorts. From our point of view, it is a legitimate criticism to note that the four motifs which Freud proposes have not been coordinated with one another (in contrast with his careful description of the position and interaction of the three levels of his interpretation of the first dream). This criticism may be of little interest to a psychoanalyst, since even a single symptom or dream element may be overdetermined without unifying or coordinating its determinants; that is, a Freudian interpretation is quite willing to accept several distinct meanings which cannot be related to one another except through the accident of their single expression. Since Freud treats separate manifest elements individually, there is no reason for him to expect their meanings to be anything but separate, at least in relation to the original manifest dream. Nor is it inconsistent, by that theory, that some elements will function in more than one meaning and yet the multiple meanings will remain unrelated, in spite of their common locus.[30] All of this is well and good within the expectations of Freudian theory. But, as the example of Dora's second dream illustrates, the standard is not sufficiently precise or demanding to exhaust the material of the dream. It is an inadequate standard from the moment the question of manifest coherence is raised. Once that question is posed, we must ask whether a single element in the dream, an image, for example, can signify two different meanings which are unrelated, and we can answer this question only by looking for relationships among the multiple meanings. If the manifest dream is coherent, the very fact that different meanings find expression in a common manifestation constitutes a relationship among them which deserves to be considered.

In the example of Dora's dream the missed opportunity is especially disappointing since the four motifs which Freud attributes to the dream share many potential relationships. If the elements of the dream are related to one another, then the motifs they represent may also be coordinated in specific and immediate ways through the coherence of the dream itself; defining those relationships ought to tell us more than we knew about the motifs. For example, if Dora seeks revenge against her father (first motif) and against Herr K. (second motif), how are the two related? Are they parallel motives? Is there a causal relationship between them, or at least a sequential one? Is one merely the duplication or vehicle for the other? If they are distinct, are their causes also distinct, and would they be satisfied by similar or different punishments? Surely the fact that, for example, the dream chooses to bury Dora's father rather than Herr K. has some bearing on questions such as these.

As a psychoanalyst, Freud may be able to answer these (and more intricate) questions by other means, without expanding or improving his interpretation of the dream. It may well be more efficient and more productive for him to leave the dream behind and turn to the wealth of other material which has accumulated during the analysis. It may even be that some of these questions would be distracting from his therapeutic goal. But the fact remains that, however successful the analysis may have been in other respects, it has not been successful in analyzing and explaining the dream itself. In order to understand the dream we must modify and supplement Freud's methods.

But Freud's misreading of the dream goes deeper. Not only has he failed to coordinate the four motifs, but the motifs themselves are suspect *as interpretations of the dream*. So, for example, we may be quite willing to grant Dora a desire for revenge on her father, but that motive is not unambiguously immanent in the dream. Even if we consider, as Freud does, that the purpose of Dora's leaving home without her parents' knowledge was to break her father's heart with grief and longing (*Dora*, pp. 97–98), the dream begins after that event and presents a subsequent (though not unrelated) subject matter. Or, if we choose to consider the father's death and burial as the fruit of Dora's revenge, how do we explain the middle section of the dream and many of the individual details of the first and third sections? Even more importantly, how can we be confident that the death of Dora's father is the result of revenge rather than a dramatization of loss? Perhaps, in some important way, Dora's father has abandoned *her*. At least we are faced with the fact that all of the material in the dream is presented in reaction to her father's death.[31]

In regard to the second motif, Dora's revenge against Herr K., we must raise a different sort of objection. This time the motif is too distant from the dream and too vaguely related to its details to be of any substantial help in reading the dream. There is no question, of course, that the dream is related to the scene by the lake, nor need there be any question of Dora's wish for revenge on Herr K.—that is immediately plausible, at least. But is that the subject of this particular dream? Perhaps the best indication of the obliqueness of the connection between this motif and the dream lies in Freud's own words: "Behind this phantasy lie concealed her thoughts of revenge against Herr K., for which she found an outlet in her behaviour to me" (*Dora*, p. 110n). Her behavior towards Freud *in the dream*? No. Freud is thinking of Dora's behavior towards him in the analysis. The dream's reference to Freud is quite different, as we will see in the next chapter.

The same criticism may be made of the third motif, Dora's love for Herr K. Here Freud bases his interpretation upon a defloration fantasy which he constructs out of elements in the first and second scenes and on the associations for the penultimate image, that of Dora walking up the stairs in order to read her big book. As we saw when we considered the images Freud connected with that fantasy, Freud has had to ignore or manipulate features of the manifest text in order to support this reading. It is not surprising, then, that the motif sheds so little light on the dream, even on those elements which Freud has linked to it.

The fourth motif is that of Dora's love for Frau K. Freud chooses to call this a homosexual love which, of course, may be misleading.[32] In a footnote contained in the postscript and probably written some time after the main body of the case history, Freud particularly emphasizes the importance of this motif, although it played no large part in his discussion of the dream:

> The longer the interval of time that separates me from the end of this analysis, the more probable it seems to me that the fault in my technique lay in this omission: I failed to discover in time and to inform the patient that her homosexual (gynaecophilic) love for Frau K. was the strongest unconscious current in her mental life. I ought to have guessed that the main source of her knowledge of sexual matters could have been no one but Frau K.—the very person who later on charged her with being interested in those same subjects. Her knowing all about such things and, at the same time, her always pretending not to know where her knowledge came from was really too remarkable. I ought to have attacked this riddle and looked for the motive of such an extraordinary piece of repression. If I had done this, the second dream would have given me my answer. The remorseless craving for revenge expressed in that dream was suited as nothing else was to conceal the current of feeling that ran contrary to it—the magnanimity with which she forgave the treachery of the friend she loved and concealed from every one the fact that it was this friend who had herself revealed to her the knowledge which had later been the ground of the accusations against her. (*Dora*, p. 120n)

The question for us is, How is such a mental current reflected in the dream? An unmistakable reference to Frau K. occurs in the idiosyncratic punctuation in Dora's mother's letter (a question mark in the middle of a sentence) which imitates the similar device in Frau K.'s letter of invitation to Dora, her invitation to the lake resort and thus to the traumatic proposal. The dream clearly alludes to Frau K. here, but in what role? She seems to have been associated with or replaced by Dora's mother, and to the extent to which that is true, she can only have been distanced and discredited by the allusion in the dream. Perhaps this is a form of revenge or rejection by the device of "exclusion from my text." If so, then the motif more nearly involved in the dream is one of revenge against Frau K. rather than repressed love for Frau K. as Freud suggests—the one, presumably, being a development of the other.

In the summary footnote Freud also calls upon the fantasy of defloration again, this time in support of Dora's homosexual love for Frau K. We have already reviewed some of the difficulties in relating this fantasy to the text of the dream; in this instance, too, Freud's invocation of the fantasy is vaguely attached to the specific elements of the dream and certainly offers no help in understanding their coherent relationship.

Again, Freud relies upon "the clearest allusions to ambiguous speeches ('Does Herr——— live here?')" (*Dora*, p. 110n). Freud's only commentary on this particular topic occurs in an earlier footnote: "In reproducing the dream Dora had forgotten one of the questions which need to be inserted into the course of the second situation of the dream. This question could only be: 'Does Herr ——— live here?' or 'Where does Herr ——— live?'" (*Dora*, p. 104, n. 2). It may occur to the reader that it is Freud, not Dora, who brings this "apparently innocent question" into the dream (*Dora*, p. 104, n. 2). Unfortunately, however, these allusions are far from clear, either in their reference to the details of the dream or in their place in the unconscious homosexual fantasy.

Finally, Freud refers in his summary footnote to Dora's sexual researches in the encyclopedia; but those researches, if they existed, are less immediately pertinent to the details of the dream than the researches conducted with Frau K., as we noted in commenting on the significance of the big book in the last scene of the dream, or even those researches conducted with Dora's earlier governess.

This is not to say that Freud is wrong about Dora's unconscious fantasies or her attitude towards Frau K., but that he is wrong about this particular dream. The dream dissociates Dora from Frau K. by a series of devices and direct contrasts. Dora's healthy walk up the stairs, her final solitude with the big book, and even the complex references to the idea of giving notice, all enforce this dissociation. In the dream Dora is, in effect, giving notice to everyone involved in the experience by the lake.

Our last criticism ought to concern Freud's most important

omission, his failure to explain his own part in the dream in spite of his recognition of the significance of his role. But this topic can best be approached in the next chapter in conjunction with our development of a full aesthetic reading which accommodates and is verified by the factual material of the case history. That coherent interpretation of the manifest text will shed clear light on Freud's role in the dream, on his conception of his role in the dream, and on the reason for his misjudgment in this matter.

Before moving on to the formulation of a comprehensive reading, we should make one final observation. In the postscript to the case history, the last section of which was probably added in 1905 (*Dora*, p. 5), Freud briefly proposes a second summary analysis of the dream, one which contradicts his earlier explanation completely:

> Years have again gone by since her visit. In the meantime the girl has married, and indeed—unless all the signs mislead me—she has married the young man who came into her associations at the beginning of the analysis of the second dream. Just as the first dream represented her turning away from the man she loved to her father—that is to say, her flight from life into disease—so the second dream announced that she was about to tear herself free from her father and had been reclaimed once more by the realities of life.   (*Dora*, p. 122)

It is obvious that this short judgment in the final sentence of the case history implies a very different view of the dream than that taken by Freud in January of 1901. The first and second dreams are now contrasted and a new topic—"that she was about to tear herself free from her father"—has been assigned to the second dream. Needless to say, the intricate analysis which Freud constructed in the case history supports this reading even less than it did his argument for the four motifs of revenge and love.[33] This last hint of Freud's is valuable, however, and a literary reading of the dream can amplify it substantially by organizing the information we have been considering.

Chapter Four

The Meaning of Dora's Dream

The Real Subject

Having focussed on Dora's second dream as a discrete imaginative production, without benefit of background or context, and having then reviewed both the factual background of the case history and Freud's interpretations, we are in a position now to attempt a synthesis which will both test and exemplify the theory that the dream is coherent at the manifest level and that a reading which ignores that coherence, as Freud's largely does, is in danger of misunderstanding the dream. Our purely literary reading produced an interpretation which was coherent and consistent, but which had not yet been related to the facts of the case. On several apparently important points the literary reading was necessarily vague or general or ambiguous, since the full value and implications of the individual elements in the dream, the personal language of symbols and references that Dora constructed, could not be clear without substantial information from the case history. Now we can assign the proper values to those terms and in so doing achieve an interpretation which is both more coherent and more comprehensive than Freud's.

It will be most convenient to proceed in two stages. First, we may formulate and describe the central topic of the dream and indicate how the dream harmonizes its details in support of that topic. We will see how, on the one hand, this controlling topic has been suggested by our literary reading and how, on the other, it provides an organization of the details of the case quite different from Freud's.

Secondly, we can address the transference meaning of the dream, understanding its relation to the dream's central topic as well as to the analytic situation—Dora's termination and her motives. This last application will serve as a final test of the importance and pertinence of an interpretation based on manifest coherence.

The key to Dora's second dream lies in two facts: first, it is not about the scene at the lake but the consequences of that experience; more particularly, the dream formulates Dora's reactions to the aftermath of the scene. Secondly, Dora's attitude towards Freud and the analysis is included in her reactions to the consequences and developments of the scene by the lake because she considered, or came to consider, her treatment by Freud (in both senses) as part of the aftermath of that traumatic incident.

That the dream is not centered on the lakeside experience is apparent in its treatment of two main characters, Herr K. and Dora's father. Herr K., in spite of his crucial role in Dora's biography, is barely included in the dream at all. He is involved in the first scene only by a very remote connection—the punctuation in Dora's mother's letter that alludes to his wife's invitation to that scene—and one which has quite another purpose than introducing him into the dream. Similarly, he is only indicated in the last scene of the dream by mechanisms (Dora's walking upstairs; the big book) which refer to his wife and which, because of their specific purposes, do not concern him in even an incidental fashion. His closest approach to any kind of presence in the dream occurs in the middle section, that which deals most directly with the lakeside temptation. But, as we have seen, it is not the proposition itself which forms the subject of that part of the dream; rather, the middle section is concerned with the process of escape and transition, and insofar as it involves Herr K., it treats Dora's escape from him. The middle scene begins its treatment of the lakeside experience immediately *after* Herr K.'s proposition, starting with Dora's first reaction to it, her symbolic inquiry for an escape ("Where is the station?") and the symbolic answer she receives ("Escape is five minutes [five days] away"). The entire section revolves around Dora's efforts to reach the station, that symbol of transition and thus escape,[1] and the most prominent character in this part of the dream is the man in the woods, a guide to the station and a would-be companion to Dora's flight.[2] Herr K. has virtually been omitted from the dream; if one of Dora's motives is to revenge herself upon him, she accomplishes this by the insult of ignoring him.

Freud, however, claims that Herr K. gains access to the dream through the figure of Dora's father: Dora's thoughts of revenge against Herr K. "lie behind" her fantasy of revenge against her father. And yet, if we examine the father's role in the dream against the background of his part in the aftermath of the lakeside scene, the real subject of the dream emerges clearly. After Herr K. had been called to account and had accused Dora of lascivious reading and an overactive imagination, Dora's father decided to believe him rather than his daughter, as he explained to Freud when he brought Dora for treatment: "'I have no doubt,' continued her father, 'that this incident is responsible for Dora's depression and irritability and suicidal ideas. She keeps pressing me to break off relations with Herr K. and more particularly with Frau K., whom she used positively to worship formerly. But that I cannot do. For, to begin with, I myself believe that Dora's tale of the man's immoral suggestions is a phantasy that has forced its way into her mind . . .'" (*Dora*, p. 26). It was, Freud notes, a most convenient course of action for preserving his relationship with Frau K. Freud also notes that this betrayal was a bitter provocation to Dora: "None of her father's actions seemed to have embittered her so much as his readiness to consider the scene by the lake as a product of her imagination. She was almost beside herself at the idea of its being supposed that she had merely fancied something on that occasion" (*Dora*, p. 46). Freud, however, will not go beyond this observation; instead, he moves on to see "what the self-reproach could be which lay behind her passionate repudiation of this explanation of the episode" (*Dora*, p. 46). Yet in discussing Dora's first dream Freud clearly exposes the motivation for this reaction to her father when he explains the course of Dora's retreat from Herr K.: "She fled *to* her father because she was afraid of the man who was pursuing her; she summoned up an infantile affection for her father so that it might protect her against her present affection for a stranger" (*Dora*, p. 86). Thus Dora's father betrayed her just when she looked to him for help. Not only that, but the manner of the betrayal carried a stinging irony which Freud never took fully into account. Dora's father betrayed her by believing the accusation that she "took no interest in anything but sexual matters" (*Dora*, p. 26). In effect, he accused her of the very fault she had so painfully resisted. She had refused the sexual temptation pointedly only to find herself accused of fabricating it by those three people who had *not* curbed their sexual interests and whose very accusation was itself a fabrication. To add to the irony, the adults' transparent motive was to perpetuate the very sort of sexual liaison which Dora had declined. It is not difficult to imagine Dora's frustration and anger, aggravated by the fact that her refusal ran counter to strong currents of real interest in Herr K. (if Freud is right). Furthermore, that refusal was based to a significant degree on her recognition that Herr K.'s proposition implied a relationship disappointingly inferior to that of her father and Frau K. and that her acceptance of his proposal might itself lead to the kind of rejection the young governess had experienced.

Frau K. was guilty of exactly the same betrayal, of course, and for the same motive. She supported her husband's accusation by providing him with the ammunition he needed, the information that Dora had been reading the *Physiology of Love*. Here, too, Dora's experience had been ironically twisted against her; her "sexual researches" with Frau K. had been turned into accusations and what had been a bond between the two had become a weapon.[3] We have already seen Freud identify Frau K. as the "main source of her [Dora's] knowledge of sexual matters" and comment on "the magnanimity with which she forgave the treachery of the friend she loved" (*Dora*, p. 120n). It is also important to realize how close their relationship had been: "The young woman and the scarcely grown girl had lived for years on a footing of the closest intimacy. When Dora stayed with the K.'s she used to share a bedroom with Frau K., and the husband used to be quartered elsewhere. She had been the wife's confidante and adviser in all the difficulties of her married life. There was nothing they had not talked about. Medea had been quite content that Creusa should make friends with her two children; and she certainly did nothing to interfere with the relations between the girl and the children's father" (*Dora*, p. 61). Dora, too, had played her cooperative part: "During all the previous years [before the scene at the lake] she had given every possible assistance to her father's relations with Frau K. She would never go to see her if she thought her father was there; but, knowing that in that case the children would have been sent out, she would turn her steps in a direction where she would be sure to meet them, and would go for a walk with them" (*Dora*, p. 36). When, after this long intimacy and complicity, Dora found herself betrayed by Frau K., who clearly preferred her father, Dora could not help but draw the parallel with the earlier situation in which a governess had similarly used her but had really only been interested in her father (*Dora*, pp. 36–37).[4]

It is these betrayals, and Dora's reaction to them, that are the subject of her second dream. Her reaction is to dissociate herself from those who have betrayed her and to return to her own privacy and her solitary quest for knowledge. She practices this dissociation most thoroughly upon her father by imagining herself living independently in a strange town, by imagining him dead, and by refusing even to attend his funeral. And since, as Freud has shown, Dora's father was to have saved her by replacing Herr K. in her affections, her disavowal of him implies a disavowal of Herr K. as well, though at a greater distance. A little more immediately, Dora disavows Frau K. by means of the allusions to her in the first and third scenes of the dream. In the first scene Frau K.'s idiosyncratic punctuation (the question mark in the middle of a sentence) is assigned to Dora's mother and appears in an invitation to return home rather than to visit the K.'s. It is as if the dream thereby substitutes Dora's mother for Frau K.[5] And the import of the invitation is ironically reversed:

Dora, in responding to it, not only returns home (coming back from the lake, as it were), but returns to a solitude unmarred by even her father's presence.

Dora's essential reaction, then, is one of rejection, aimed particularly at her father who, in so many ways, figured at the beginning and ending points in her long drama of involvement.[6] In the formulation of the dream, that reaction is played out through the major themes of knowledge and time, which organize references to the key events involved in Dora's reaction. We said earlier that the dream offers knowledge about the way time leads to knowledge. We might restate that summary now by saying that the dream achieves knowledge by demonstrating the relationships among different periods of time. Specific points of the past, present, and future are identified and correlated in the structure of the dream as Dora moves through its ambiguous process of rejection. In light of the available biographical information, we can see that the paradoxical treatment of chronology in the dream—the movement which is simultaneously backwards and forwards in time—dramatizes and explains Dora's progressive rejection of her betrayers.

A number of ambiguities are immediately clarified if we realize that the three-part structure of the dream enacts a double chronology in order to relate the past to the future and in order to describe a future, Dora's goal in the dream, which can recover certain aspects of her past while excluding and rejecting others. The double chronology is apparent in the fact that each of the three sections of the dream refers to two separate events or periods in Dora's life. Altogether, then, the dream refers to six major periods:

1. *Before the Lake*
   The period before the incident at the lake, characterized by Dora's strong relationship with Frau K., her as yet unresolved relationship with Herr K., and the transference of her love for her father at least partly into those relationships.
2. *The Lake*
   Herr K.'s insulting proposition and Dora's initial reactions, up to the time of her betrayal.

3. *The Betrayal*
Herr K.'s accusation, Frau K.'s implicit support of it, Dora's father's decision to believe them rather than her, and Dora's reactions to these betrayals.
4. *The Analysis*
Dora's treatment by Freud two and a half years after the lakeside scene; she considers the analysis the last link in the chain of betrayal which followed that scene.
5. *After the Analysis*
The period which will immediately follow Dora's termination of the analysis, represented by an image of her isolation.
6. *The Marriage*
A vague image of the more distant future, perhaps involving the young engineer; only weakly implied by the dream.

Against this chronology we can test each of the three scenes and, in so doing, describe the function of the major images in the dream's process of rejection. Thus the first scene refers to both *The Betrayal* and *The Marriage*. Its reference to *The Betrayal* is made by the fact of Dora's departure from her home and by the announcement of her father's death. More precisely, these elements express Dora's reaction to her father's disloyalty; as we noted earlier, the two events are related acts of dissociation motivated by Dora's reaction, including her disillusionment. Dora's reaction to the betrayal is also evident in the letter from her mother which reverses Frau K.'s invitation to the lake resort; the letter calls her back from her involvement with the affairs of Frau K. and her father (her mother being the ideal instrument for this), inviting her to a home where her father will be absent. Dora's repudiation, furthermore, involves her leaving "without her parents' knowledge" in the sense that they will not understand or share this development of hers, in the sense that she no longer wishes to have knowledge of or contact with her parents, especially her father, and in the self-justifying sense that she has not had the sexual "knowledge" her father has enjoyed with Frau K. This last sense refers directly, of course, to the accusation, accepted by her father, that Dora produced a lascivious fantasy rather than rejecting a real temptation.

At the same time, however, the first scene also refers to *The Marriage*, a vague expectation of the sexual life that will eventually replace the network of relationships which Dora lost in the aftermath of the lakeside scene. This reference is generated by the strange town and its monument. In effect, Dora has left her father to consider, in both senses of the word, the monument in the square; if this is read sexually, then we find Dora confronting the idea of male sexuality at a general level or, perhaps, in specific relation to the potential suitor whose postcard from and of a strange town constituted the day residue of this image.[7]

It is interesting that these two chronological references are presented in reverse order in the dream. The town and the monument, projecting furthest into the future, appear first. In fact, the prospect they imply is in some ways dependent upon the symbolic death which follows them in the dream, at least to the extent that Dora must first detach herself from her father before she can begin new involvements. The order of references also seems backwards if we consider that they are symbolically complementary: a marriage would replace Dora's relationship with her father and a husband would displace him to a significant degree. Both symbols, then, deal with Dora's repudiation of her father, and their reversed chronology merely begins the dream's paradoxical treatment of time, described in our literary analysis. In specific terms, this section of the dream draws a relationship between the betrayal and its future consequences by showing an imagined outcome to Dora's reaction to the betrayal.

The middle scene, likewise, makes a double reference. Most obviously it hearkens back to Herr K.'s lakeside proposal—or rather, to Dora's immediate reaction to that proposition and to the five-day period of tension which followed. Several details from that period are directly incorporated into the scene, as we have noted, and the section as a whole treats the idea of transition or escape. A second reference is made by one of those reproduced elements, however; the man Dora meets in the woods, as we have several times implied, partly represents Freud, and so this section of the dream also refers to *The Analysis* as well as to *The Lake*. The anonymous and ambiguous stranger in the woods who offers Dora both directions and company for her escape is the character she refuses and the character who appears in the dream as an alternate or substitute for her father.[8] But it is his answer to Dora's question which alludes most clearly to the analysis: "two and a half hours" was the length of time remaining in the analysis when Dora presented the dream to Freud, and two and a half years was the time between the lakeside incident and the termination of the analysis (from the end of June 1898 to the end of December 1900). In its revised form of "two," the figure also refers to the giving of notice which we discussed earlier, including the notice Dora gave Freud by means of this dream (thus the self-reflexive dimension that we noted when examining this middle scene of the dream in chapter 2). The connection is strengthened by the fact that much of Freud's analysis dealt with the scene at the lake and its implications and by the consideration that Dora must have regarded his offer of help (i.e., the analysis) as implicated in the aftermath of that scene, an extension of her father's unwillingness to believe her (he "handed her over" to Freud so that Freud might convince her it was all a fantasy), as we will see more clearly when we examine the transference meaning of the dream.

The third scene refers to the two chronological periods that remain, *Before the Lake* and *After the Analysis*. On the one hand, this scene carries Dora back to a time before the temptation incident by returning her to the home of her youth and by inverting key images from that earlier period (she reads the book, but alone instead of with Frau K.; she walks healthily up the stairs). On the other hand, the last scene alludes to the period immediately *After the Analysis*: Dora sees herself pursuing her studies, including her self-study, alone, having cut herself off from all the principals of the betrayal including, finally, Freud.

At this point, the significance of the book, her final goal in the dream, is much clearer. The book has to do with the betrayals, of course, but Dora approaches it here in the dream with other references also in mind. In arriving at the book, she moves backwards, in the sense that she must study the past, not only in order to understand the trauma and its aftermath but in order to investigate and perhaps begin to repair the psychical foundations that were undermined by the betrayals. In a sense, Dora must reread the book she studied with Frau K., but now she must do it alone in order to recover and reevaluate the material of the past and in order to establish her solitary independence from those who betrayed her. She must continue on alone and continuing involves a reexamination of the past, also to be carried out alone. Much of the material to be reexamined is sexual. The shock of the betrayals forces her to investigate the sexual motives and involvements that led up to them, and so she returns, as it were, to Frau K.'s book, albeit with new eyes. The book also invites Dora to study her own past sexuality and motives, again for purposes of reevaluation and, possibly, future reconstruction. Finally, the book refers to her current studies, her substitute for social intercourse and the temporary replacement in her life for the involvements that turned out so badly.[9]

Like the first section, the third links distinct time periods in order to show the relationship between them. In fact, the two time references in the third section are almost overlaid, one on top of the other, instead of being attached to separate subsections and images as they were in the first scene. That is, both parts of this section (Dora's arrival home; her reading of the big book) refer to both of the time periods involved, ambiguously. The sharp distinction of chronologies is lost, and what results is a fusion of past and future. We noted in the literary analysis that Dora's destination in the dream is a future including her past. Now we might rephrase that observation by saying that Dora's future, in the dream, requires a revision of her past, a reconstruction. So she returns home, after having moved away, and that seems like a return to the past except that the home she returns to has changed: her father is dead. Likewise, she reads the big book again, but alone instead of with Frau K. It would be fair to say that what had started out as an expression of Dora's reaction to the betrayals, a dramatization of her repudiation of the characters involved, has developed into a program for her future, however limited.

The knowledge of time we discussed in our literary reading thus assumes a more specific character. It consists in knowledge about how certain periods in Dora's history relate to one another, or could. Her reaction to the betrayals could free her for future love, according to the dream. Her repudiation of her father must be repeated (she feels) in her refusal of Freud, and that refusal will constitute the last of her reactions to the last of her betrayers. Her independence after the analysis will allow her to return to and revise her past.[10]

A simple schema will illustrate the paradoxical chronology more clearly:

	Chronology A	Chronology B
Scene 1	*The Betrayal*	*The Marriage*
Scene 2	*The Lake*	*The Analysis*
Scene 3	*Before the Lake*	*After the Analysis*

Now it is particularly evident why Dora seems to be moving forwards and backwards at the same time as she progresses through the dream. On the one hand, Chronology A carries her backwards, step by step, in due order, until she reaches a modified past which is free of the difficulties of the present and recent past. On the other hand, Chronology B carries her forward, beginning with a vague reference to the distant future, the barely imagined time when she will be free of the past and involved in entirely new sexual interests, as represented by the allusion to her potential suitor. This is followed by the allusion to the analysis and Dora's intention of terminating it, the step she must take in the present in order to begin to move towards her imagined future. After this the dream moves forward again to the immediate future, the period that will follow her termination of the analysis and precede the distant, imagined future. This chronological pattern follows a 3-1-2 order, as if it were suggesting a distant goal and then returning to the present (the analysis) to begin a movement towards that distant goal.[11] Here too, in a different way, Dora must go back in order to go forward.

In this coherent and complex movement neither love nor revenge appears foremost. However important those motives have been for Dora, they are not the primary subject of this dream. Revenge is overshadowed by escape and transition; love, spoiled by betrayal, has yielded to independence and solitude.[12] The past, if the dream could have its way, would remold itself into a future.

The Transference

One major topic remains. It has become increasingly clear that Dora's repudiation of Freud constituted, in her mind, the last of her reactions to her betrayers. The dream seems to imply that she needed to cut herself off from him, as well as from them, if she were to advance into her future. Why, precisely, did Dora terminate the analysis? In a sense this topic offers itself as a final and intriguing test of our literary reading, as well as a kind of pivotal example to illustrate the different implications of the literary reading and the psychoanalytic one. The example is all the more interesting in this particular instance because we know by now that the transference significance of the dream is one of its important dimensions, that Freud underemphasized that aspect of the dream, both in the analysis and in his interpretation of the dream itself, and that the failure of the analysis was at least partly due to the lost emphasis. It would be a most interesting commentary on the pertinence of our literary reading if it not only accommodated a transference interpretation but also helped to explain Freud's shortcomings here. In this case, at least, that is exactly what we may expect of it. The fact of the matter is that Freud made the same mistake in interpreting the dream that he made in interpreting Dora.[13] The dream corrects Freud's mistake by presenting Dora's viewpoint on the subject and by expressing her reaction to Freud's error.[14]

Freud recognizes that the dream refers to him and acknowledges the allusion to the analysis made by the phrase "two hours" in the middle section, but he is unable to develop a consistent and detailed reading of this aspect of the dream. He is as puzzled about its transference meaning as he is about Dora's decision to quit the analysis, and he recognizes that those two topics are closely connected. It is not until the postscript, however, that he turns his attention to the transference:

> In Dora's second dream there are several clear allusions to transference. At the time she was telling me the dream I was still unaware (and did not learn until two days later) that we had only *two hours* more work before us. This was the same length of time which she had spent in front of the Sistine Madonna, and which (by making a correction and putting "two hours" instead of "two and a half hours") she had taken as the length of the walk which she had not made round the lake. . . . The treatment, she had thought, was too long for her; she would never have the patience to wait so long. And yet in the first few weeks she had had discernment enough to listen without making any such objections when I informed her that her complete recovery would require perhaps a year. Her refusing in the dream to be accompanied, and preferring to go alone, also originated from her visit to the gallery at Dresden, and I was myself to experience them on the appointed day. What they meant was, no doubt: "Men are all so detestable that I would rather not marry. This is my revenge."
>
> (*Dora*, pp. 119–120)

That last summary evaluation, even if it were accurate, would stop a good deal short of explaining the dream's treatment of the transference. But Freud has commented on the transference itself in a peculiar way; he acknowledges its part in the failure of the analysis, but cannot understand how or why the transference misfired:

> I was deaf to this first note of warning [i.e., the first dream], thinking I had ample time before me. . . . In this way the transference took me unawares, and, because of the unknown quantity in me which reminded Dora of Herr K., she took her revenge on me as she wanted to take her revenge on him, and deserted me as she believed herself to have been deceived

and deserted by him. Thus she *acted out* an essential part of her recollections and phantasies instead of reproducing it in the treatment. What this unknown quantity was I naturally cannot tell. I suspect that it had to do with money, or with jealousy of another patient who had kept up relations with my family after her recovery. (*Dora*, p. 119)

Two points emerge: Freud regards the transference as involving Herr K̲., and he is unable to determine its basis. The speculative motives he offers at the end of this passage are poor guesses. Neither finances nor jealousy of another patient are mentioned elsewhere in the case history, nor can they be related to any of the major topics of Freud's analysis. Even if they were pertinent, they would only explain Dora's motive for revenging herself on Freud, not the basis of her transference from Herr K. to Freud. They seem to have nothing to do with Herr K. at all. In short, this indecisive speculation is a weak attempt at a deus ex machina, one which Freud himself seems to put little stock in, and it ought to arouse our suspicions almost as much as Freud's claim that "naturally" he did not know the basis of Dora's transference. On the next page he thinks an entirely different factor may be involved, and a long footnote presents the alternate theory: Freud speculates that his mistake was in underestimating Dora's "homosexual love" for Frau K. But the point is not developed in a sustained way, nor is it coordinated with his other speculations on this topic.

It is odd that Freud recognizes the significance of this phenomenon and yet cannot formulate a convincing hypothesis on the subject.[15] It is also odd that he reacts so intensely to Dora's decision not to continue with him; in his concluding description of their final session, his rhetoric betrays his strong emotion:[16]

> Dora had listened to me without any of her usual contradictions. She seemed to be moved; she said good-bye to me very warmly, with the heartiest wishes for the New Year, and— came no more. . . . I knew Dora would not come back again. Her breaking off so unexpectedly, just when my hopes of a

successful termination of the treatment were at their highest, and her thus bringing those hopes to nothing—this was an unmistakable act of vengeance on her part. Her purpose of self-injury also profited by this action. No one who, like me, conjures up the most evil of those half-tamed demons that inhabit the human breast, and seeks to wrestle with them, can expect to come through the struggle unscathed.

(*Dora*, pp. 108–109)[17]

From this last sentence Freud goes on to imagine other courses of action he might have taken to avert this disappointment and then, oddly, wonders how the scene at the lake might have turned out had Herr K. known what he knows about Dora's deeper motives.

This last topic introduces another category of surprising attitudes on Freud's part, namely, those instances in which he offers the most unexpected interpretations of Dora's reactions. These all have to do with Herr K. and Dora's father, and most of them with the former. The instance just referred to is a good example: "Nor do I know whether Herr K. would have done any better if it had been revealed to him that the slap Dora gave him by no means signified a final 'No' on her part, but that it expressed the jealousy which had lately been roused in her, while her strongest feelings were still on his side. If he had disregarded that first 'No,' and had continued to press his suit with a passion which left room for no doubts, the result might very well have been a triumph of the girl's affection for him over all her internal difficulties" (*Dora*, pp. 109–110). This is surely unexpected on Freud's part; it is almost as if he is envisioning the lakeside scene from Herr K.'s point of view. Certainly, for the moment, he has lost sight of his patient. And it is not the first time. Earlier, after affirming his acceptance of Dora's version of the facts of the lakeside incident, he lapses suddenly into Herr K.'s viewpoint: "No sooner had she grasped Herr K.'s intention than, without letting him finish what he had to say, she had given him a slap in the face and hurried away. Her behaviour must have seemed as incomprehensible to the man after she had left him as to us" (*Dora*, p. 46). Yet Dora's behavior was anything but incomprehensible, as Freud himself later discovers (*Dora*, p. 106). But along the same lines, Freud allows himself to make the unusual implication that Dora was hasty and that Herr K.'s proposition might have been of substantial interest to her:

> You took it that he was only waiting till you were grown up enough to be his wife. . . . You have not even got the right to assert that it was out of the question for Herr K. to have had any such intention; you have told me enough about him that points directly towards his having such an intention. Nor does his behaviour at L—— contradict this view. After all, you did not let him finish his speech and do not know what he meant to say to you. Incidentally, the scheme would by no means have been so impracticable. . . . Indeed, if your temptation at L—— had had a different upshot, this [i.e., marrying Herr K.] would have been the only possible solution for all the parties concerned. (*Dora*, p. 108)

Here, too, Freud takes a surprising approach to the subject. He is forgetting what he elsewhere knows: Dora was influenced by her knowledge, recently acquired, that Herr K. had made a similar speech to his governess, had succeeded in seducing her, and then had spurned her. The point, then, is not whether Dora secretly hoped to marry Herr K. some day—if she did, then the warning implicit in the governess' unfortunate experience would have been all the sharper.[18] Rather, in this passage Freud fails to see that Herr K.'s proposal must have appeared to Dora as a repetition of his treatment of the governess, especially since he used the same language ("he got nothing from his wife") that Dora knew he had used to persuade her predecessor.[19] Whether Dora hoped for marriage or whether she had never consciously entertained the idea, Herr K.'s proposition was insulting and demeaning.[20] Freud is wrong here: Dora did know what Herr K. intended to say to her because she had heard it before—from the seduced governess.

This failure on Freud's part to take account of motives of Dora's which he elsewhere identifies and his intermittent lapses into Herr K.'s viewpoint leave him in confusion about Dora's reaction to the proposal by the lake. Whereas he makes the necessary connection with the governess's experience at one point (*Dora*, p. 106), at another point he is completely perplexed: "The question then arises: If Dora loved Herr K., what was the reason for her refusing him in the scene by the lake? Or at any rate, why did her refusal take such a brutal form, as though she were embittered against him? And how could a girl who was in love feel insulted by a proposal which was made in a manner neither tactless nor offensive?" (*Dora*, p. 38, n. 2). It is difficult to know what to say about this. The reason for Dora's refusal ought to be crystal clear, and it was precisely because she was embittered that she reacted so strongly. Under the circumstances, it is very difficult to see how this sixteen-year-old's slap in the face can be described as "brutal."[21]

That adjective might be applied with a little more justice to Freud's handling of Dora's first affront from Herr K.:

> When the first difficulties of the treatment had been overcome, Dora told me of an earlier episode with Herr K., which was even better calculated to act as a sexual trauma. She was fourteen years old at the time. Herr K. had made an arrangement with her and his wife that they should meet him one afternoon at his place of business in the principal square of B—— so as to have a view of a church festival. He persuaded his wife, however, to stay at home, and sent away his clerks, so that he was alone when the girl arrived. When the time for the procession approached, he asked the girl to wait for him at the door which opened on to the staircase leading to the upper story, while he pulled down the outside shutters. He then came back, and, instead of going out by the open door, suddenly clasped the girl to him and pressed a kiss upon her lips. This was surely just the situation to call up a distinct feeling of sexual excitement in a girl of fourteen who had never before been approached. But Dora had at that moment a violent feeling of disgust . . .   (*Dora*, pp. 27–28)

In the next paragraph, Freud begins his discussion of the "reversal of affect," "In this scene . . . the behaviour of this child of fourteen was already entirely and completely hysterical." Her reaction is all the more surprising to him because, as he mentions in a footnote on the following page, "I happen to know Herr K., . . . and he was still quite young and of prepossessing appearance." At the very least we might take exception to Freud's tone here, and in light of the other instances in the case history in which he has seemed to understand Herr K.'s interests more vividly than Dora's, we may wonder if his clinical evaluation here is perfectly balanced.[22]

So far, then, we have very good evidence on two points that can hardly be unrelated. On the one hand, Freud reflects back on the analysis and speculates that its failure was due in some measure to his difficulty with Dora's transference from Herr K. to himself, although he is unable to guess the basis of that transference.[23] On the other hand, in several striking passages of the case history he shows a surprising receptivity to Herr K.'s viewpoint, even at the cost of misunderstanding Dora's.[24] These lapses in Freud's viewpoint should make us skeptical of his explanation of the transference. To what extent was Herr K. involved in Dora's transference, particularly as it relates to her dream? We have already noted Herr K.'s severely restricted role in the manifest dream. He has, in effect, been replaced by Dora's father, at least in terms of his prominence. If the dream makes an important reference to Freud, it would seem more likely to do that through the figure of Dora's father rather than through Herr K.; and Freud's sympathy for Herr K. suggests that Freud is overestimating that character's role in the dream as he is in Dora's transference.

There are good reasons to consider the relationship between Freud and Dora's father in the dream. In the first place, Freud acknowledges that this relationship played an important role in the analysis: "At the beginning it was clear that I was replacing her father in her imagination, which was not unlikely, in view of the difference between our ages. She was even constantly comparing me with him consciously, and kept anxiously trying to make sure whether I was being quite straightforward with her, for her father 'always preferred secrecy and roundabout ways'" (*Dora*, p. 118). The second sentence here contains a valuable hint—a comparison of Freud with her father raised the question of straightforwardness—to which we will have to return later.[25] On the comparison itself, however, we recall that Freud figured in Dora's first dream, which he also understood as a warning to him that she intended to abandon the analysis, and in which Dora's father occupied the central role.

Freud is also linked with Dora's father by the circumstances of the analysis. When Dora's father first brought her to Freud, it was in the hope that Freud would "bring her to reason" and convince her that the lakeside incident had only been imagined (*Dora*, p. 26). Initially, at least, Freud must have seemed to be a tool for reinforcing the adults' betrayal of Dora by accusing her of lascivious fantasies. Later, Freud makes a passing reference to the fact that it was only Dora's father who made her come to the analysis, even after it was well started (*Dora*, p. 70, n. 2). Certainly in repudiating the analysis, Dora was indirectly repudiating her father, thus manipulating the connection between the two.

Finally, there is the strong implication that Freud's most immanent presence in the second dream is by means of the character Dora meets in the woods. This man encounters Dora after the lakeside temptation and offers her directions and company. She refuses him, as she finally did Freud. But the man in the woods functions as a counterpart to Dora's father in the dream; his only connection with Herr K. is that he offers Dora assistance in her escape from Herr K. Insofar as the dream alludes to Freud through this character, it is seeing Freud in relation to Dora's father. Dora's repudiation of Freud is, in a sense, more current than that of her father, more direct, and leads her finally to the solitary independence of the last scene—in all respects, that is, Dora's refusal of the man in the woods most closely resembles her refusal of Freud.

If we now recall the main subject of the dream, the reason why Dora repudiated her father in it, we will be in a position to draw these several lines of thought together. Because Freud sees the transference, at this point in the analysis, too much in terms of Herr K. and because he overestimates Herr K.'s importance in the dream, he fails to see his own function there. The dream is centered on Dora's father, not on Herr K., and it is chiefly through his presence (and that of the complementary character in the woods) that it makes its reference to Freud. Furthermore, the specific subject of the dream is Dora's reaction to (principally) her father's betrayal of her, a betrayal which consisted in his not believing her. If the parallel with Freud holds, then Dora must be reacting, in the dream, to a similar betrayal by Freud, as it appears to her. Her reaction is the same: she cuts herself off from Freud as she has from her father, and so the dream makes its reference to the termination of the analysis in the context of her father's metaphorical death.[26]

But in what way did Freud betray Dora? Or in what way did he seem to, from her point of view? The answer to that question lies partly in our observations on his apparent preference for Herr K.'s point of view, rather than Dora's, at several points in the analysis. Freud betrayed Dora, as it seemed to her, in exactly the same way her father had, that is, by not believing her.[27] He did not doubt her description of the literal events of the incident by the lake, of course. But in other important respects he gave the appearance of doubting her. His entire interpretation of the second dream, for example, denies Dora's claim (and the dream's) that she has put her love for Herr K. (and for her father and Frau K. as well) behind her.[28] His unearthing of unconscious fantasies, however accurate, bore too close a resemblance to the accusation made against her by Herr K. and her father. Freud, too, was accusing her of lascivious fantasies. Even in some of the details of the analysis, Freud's goals and procedures struck an unfortunate analogy with aspects of Dora's betrayal by her father and her friends.[29] Thus, for example, Freud accused her of sexual researches in an encyclopedia (an event which is never actually recovered from Dora's memory) whereas Herr K. accused her of sexual researches in Mantegazza. Freud's suggestion that Dora might have been better off accepting Herr K.'s proposal could have seemed to Dora like another rationalization in the interest of preserving the liaison between her father and Frau K. But probably more important than any of these considerations is the fact that Freud did not entirely believe or accept Dora's account of the lakeside scene. That is, he never fully credited her motive for refusing Herr K., never gave sufficient weight to the influence of the example of the unfortunate governess on Dora's evaluation of and reaction to Herr K.'s proposition.³⁰ In this way—as in the several others we have just reviewed—Freud gave the appearance of aligning himself with Herr K. against her, which is exactly what her father had done.³¹ Surely Dora understood her father's expectations with regard to the analysis ("He had given his support to the treatment so long as he could hope that I should 'talk' Dora out of her belief that there was something more than a friendship between him and Frau K." [*Dora*, p. 109]). In Dora's eyes, Freud was simply the latest in the parade of her betrayers, and she dealt with him as she had with the others.³²

From this point of view, Freud's final comment on the dream, that it "announced that she was about to tear herself free from her father and had been reclaimed once more by the realities of life," seems apt and credible. As the dream promised, Dora's future lay in her past, and the passage of time would be the vehicle of her progress towards that future. Later events seem to have borne this out, as became apparent when Dora paid a round of visits to the principal characters in her drama in order to set things right. Fifteen months after she terminated the analysis, she visited Freud and supplied him with the epilogue to her story:

> For four or five weeks after stopping the treatment she had been "all in a muddle," as she said. A great improvement had then set in; her attacks had become less frequent and her spirits had risen. In the May of that year one of the K.'s two children (it had always been delicate) had died. She took the opportunity of their loss to pay them a visit of condolence, and they received her as though nothing had happened in the last three years. She made it up with them, she took her revenge on them, and she brought her own business to a satisfactory conclusion. To the wife she said: "I know you have an affair with my father"; and the other did not deny it. From the husband she drew an admission of the scene by the lake which he had disputed, and brought the news of her vindication home to her father. Since then she had not resumed her relations with the family. (*Dora*, p. 121)

In a sense, Dora also seems to have settled accounts with Freud on this visit, though in a rather different way. She reported a new symptom to him, "a right-sided facial neuralgia, from which she was now suffering day and night" (*Dora*, p. 121). Freud discovered that the symptom had been going on for two weeks and noted that it had been two weeks since Dora had read a newspaper article concerning him, a fact which she confirmed. It seems that Dora brought a last, clearly symbolic symptom to him. In this matter, I think Freud once again misplaces his emphasis: "Her alleged facial neuralgia was thus a self-punishment—remorse at having once given Herr K. a box on the ear, and at having transferred her feelings of revenge on to me. I do not know what kind of help she wanted from me, but I promised to forgive her for having deprived me of the satisfaction of affording her a far more radical cure for her troubles" (*Dora*, p. 122). Dora regretted the aftermath of her slap more than the slap itself, no doubt; and perhaps the symbolic slap in the face which she inflicted on herself had something to do with a reevaluation of Freud's analysis, and of his help, however reluctantly and briefly she accepted it at the time. After all, what Dora brought to Freud on this April 1 visit was news of his patient's improvement, though more through her own treatment than his, as she may have thought. She had justified herself, had proven she was right. The date itself, not surprisingly, aroused Freud's suspicions, especially since "times and dates, as we know, were never without significance for her" (*Dora*, p. 120). So the choice of April 1 was part of Dora's message, as was the two-week duration of her new symptom, for two weeks was the period of the symbolic notices she had given all her betrayers. We might guess, then, that Dora was serving notice on herself as well as on Freud and that her self-punishment suggested the cost of being right. Perhaps, too, the punishment was born of guilt as well as regret—not for her revenge on Herr K. and on Freud, and not for refusing Herr K. either. There was something else Dora might punish herself for, especially on April Fool's Day, as the next chapter suggests.

Chapter Five

The Ideology of Sex

The Feminine Mystery

When Dora returned to Freud for her last visit, he said that he did not know what she wanted of him. From the beginning of the analysis, Dora had her secrets; though Freud discovered some of them, both during and after those eleven weeks, others escaped him, as this comment on the last page of the case history implies.

Some of Dora's secrets were pathological and some were feminine. In the same year that Dora's case was finally published (1905), *Three Essays on the Theory of Sexuality* also appeared, and in that work Freud commented that the erotic life of women, "partly owing to the stunting effect of civilized conditions and partly owing to their conventional secretiveness and insincerity—is still veiled in an impenetrable obscurity." Even as late as his essay on "Female Sexuality" (1931) Freud noted the obscurity of female sexual development, particularly in the crucial preoedipal period: "Our insight into this early, pre-Oedipus, phase in girls," he writes, "comes to us as a surprise, like the discovery, in another field, of the Minoan-Mycenean civilization behind the civilization of Greece. Everything in the sphere of this first attachment to the mother seemed to me so difficult to grasp in analysis . . . that it was as if it had succumbed to an especially inexorable repression. . . . Nor have I succeeded in seeing my way through any case completely, and I shall therefore confine myself to reporting the most general findings and shall give only a few examples of the new ideas which I have arrived at. Among these is a suspicion that this phase of attachment to the mother is especially intimately related to the aetiology of hysteria."[1] In his treatment of Dora, two particular secrets made her especially mysterious to Freud; one of them, her "homosexual" love for Frau K., he discovered after he last saw her. The other, the importance of Dora's mother in her history before and after her analysis, escaped Freud entirely.

Both of these topics have been emphasized recently by writers committed to what may broadly be termed a feminist perspective. Since Freud's theories about and attitudes toward female sexuality are problematical and since this case history is one of the principal documents on the subject, naturally feminists interested in Freud are also interested in Dora.[2] Their emphasis has helped to restore a further dimension to our understanding of Dora, and it has also raised additional questions about her. If we pursue some of these questions, we will find a point of intersection between our work with Dora's dreams and these two feminist topics: Dora's first dream, which we have only briefly considered thus far, can provide an important clue to the relationship of these two aspects of Dora's experience and the relationship between her feminine and her pathological secrets. Before we begin that subject, however, we should digress for a few moments in order to clear the ground a bit, for the feminist issues of Dora's case have attracted a good deal of the growing commentary on the case history, not all of it equally helpful in understanding either Dora or her dreams. A brief review of some of these topics will form a helpful background to our own selected interests.

Dora as Victim

In one respect Dora's case has turned out to be a disappointing document for feminist thinkers, and here the dreams can be of little help. As our quotation from "On Female Sexuality" suggests, much of the theory of female sexual development has centered on the importance of preoedipal relationships. Freud, however, gives us almost no information about Dora before the age of eight—partly, no doubt, because he had not yet recognized the importance of this period and partly because the brevity of the truncated analysis did not afford sufficient opportunity for the recovery of more early material.[3] As a result, correlations between Dora's early childhood and her adolescent symptoms must remain very generalized and almost entirely speculative.

That restriction aside, there are several more specific questions which can be addressed. One general effect of feminist attention to the case has been a greater effort to see things from Dora's point of view and to take a more sympathetic attitude towards her difficulties—a sympathy first introduced by the work of Erik Erikson and Steven Marcus to which I have already referred.[4] The other side of this coin has also been turned: there has been an effort by some writers to be less sympathetic to Freud and to his difficulties.[5]

It is quite obvious from our current perspective that Dora's situation constitutes a dramatic example of both the depth and the pervasiveness of what can only be called anti-feminine assumptions and of the extraordinarily limiting and debilitating effect those assumptions could have on a young woman. Dora's difficulties were due in large part to the powerful attitudes of her milieu that tolerated the sort of sexual involvements in which she was trapped. Once she was trapped, those same attitudes left her very few options. Her range of possible reactions was so narrow and so unsatisfactory that it is impossible not to regard her hysteria with real sympathy. Clearly, Dora's experience belongs in the canon of documents that support recent efforts to identify and evaluate sexist attitudes.

There is a certain point, therefore, to the complaint that Freud discounted the influence of external factors in his analysis, that, in Salvatore Maddi's words, "Freud was trying to force her to adjust to an intolerable and destructive situation."[6] Erik Erikson also emphasizes the importance of Dora's environment in her illness and the way in which her experience would have been especially frustrating for an adolescent.[7] But Juliet Mitchell has pointed out that Freud was not entirely insensitive to these issues—"Freud introduces the psychical complex that he is to reveal by the sort of sociological comment on families that would warm the heart of many a radical therapist today"—and she quotes his own statement on the subject: "It follows from the nature of the facts which form the material of psycho-analysis that we are obliged to pay as much attention in our case histories to the purely human and social circumstances of our patients as to the somatic data and the symptoms of the disorder. Above all, our interest will be directed towards their family circumstances—and not only, as will be seen later, for the purpose of enquiring into their heredity" (*Dora*, p. 18).[8] It would be more appropriate, then, to criticize Freud for failing to take full account of the external factors as they were refracted in the experience of his patient and the details of his case, not for ignoring them altogether.

For important as Dora's circumstances were, of themselves they throw only a limited light on her case, on the specifics of her symptoms and reactions and on the details of her analysis. Thus Mitchell criticizes the neo-Freudian feminists who would shift the emphasis of their analysis almost entirely to external factors: "Feminist criticisms of Freud claim that he was denying what really happens, and that the women he analysed were simply responding to really oppressive conditions. But there is no such thing as a simple response to reality. External reality has to be 'acquired.' To deny that there is anything other than external reality gets us back to the same proposition: it is a denial of the unconscious." Speaking in another connection, Mitchell states, "In this instance, as in others, there is nothing neither true nor false but thinking makes it so, and if patriarchal thought is dominant then femininity will reflect that system: 'nature' is not exempt from its representation in mental life."[9] The point, therefore, is that Dora's milieu cannot fully explain the specifics of Dora's experience and motives and her individual reactions to that milieu; it cannot supply answers to the questions raised by Dora's symptoms or Freud's explanation of them. A recommendation such as Maddi's that Freud should have simply told Dora she was right or should have "precipitated a confrontation among them all in his presence, or even counseled her to leave her corrupt home for college" misses the point entirely.[10] In fact, the very argument that the external factors which influenced Dora were part and parcel of her cultural milieu made the prospect of altering that environment, as objectionable as it was, patently unrealistic, and this is the real point to be made in a feminist analysis of Dora's circumstances. Nor are attempts to idolize Dora very credible. While there is no doubt that she was a victim—of her age and her sex, of her father's intrigues and those of the K.'s, and, in an entirely different sense, of Freud's theories—there is equal certainty that she was not entirely an innocent, that she was more than an accomplice in her own illness.

Nor was Freud entirely a villain. A comparison of his methods of treatment with others common in the late nineteenth century is a sobering antidote to too facile a criticism of his behavior.[11] It is worth noting, in addition, that his treatment of Dora may have been uncharacteristic in some ways, presumably due to the influence of particular factors, not the least of which was his countertransference. Steven Marcus has called attention to a number of parallels between Dora's case and that of "Katharina" in *Studies on Hysteria* (1895) and has suggested that Freud took the latter for an inappropriate model when treating Dora.[12] But if we compare Freud's attitudes in the two instances, a striking contrast emerges. In the earlier document he is sympathetic and gentle. When Katharine reports that her uncle made sexual advances towards her—by getting into bed with her—and that she "defended herself" (in Freud's terminology) without fully realizing the sexual nature of the advance, Freud takes her at her word instead of judging her hysterical because she did not respond sexually. When the exact sensation of the physical contact becomes an issue, Freud proceeds in a manner and tone very different from that of his interrogation of Dora:

> "Tell me just one more thing. You're a grown-up girl now and know all sorts of things . . ."
> "Yes, now I am."
> "Tell me just one thing. What part of his body was it that you felt that night."
> But she gave me no more definite answer. She smiled in an

> embarrassed way, as though she had been found out. . . . I could imagine what the tactile sensation was which she had later learnt to interpret. Her facial expression seemed to me to be saying that she supposed that I was right in my conjecture. . . .
> I hope this girl, whose sexual sensibility had been injured at such an early age, derived some benefit from our conversation. I have not seen her since.[13]

Differences in the circumstances notwithstanding, there is a remarkable contrast of attitudes here, though not really more striking than the contrast between Freud's attitude towards Dora and towards the young lesbian he treated twenty years later. She, too, was eighteen when she saw him. After commenting on the improbability of his satisfying her parents' intentions and the unfavorable conditions for analysis which her case involved, he deals with the girl's own intentions:

> At a certain period, not long after the treatment had begun, the girl brought a series of dreams which . . . anticipated the cure of the inversion [i.e., her homosexuality] through the treatment, expressed her joy over the prospects in life that would then be opened before her, confessed her longing for a man's love and for children, and so might have been welcomed as a gratifying preparation for the desired change. The contradiction between them and the girl's utterances in waking life at the time was very great. . . . Warned through some slight impression or other, I told her one day that I did not believe these dreams, that I regarded them as false or hypocritical, and that she intended to deceive me just as she habitually deceived her father. I was right; after I had made this clear, this kind of dream ceased. But I still believe that, beside the intention to mislead me, the dreams partly expressed the wish to win my favour; they were also an attempt to gain my interest and my good opinion—perhaps in order to disappoint me all the more thoroughly later on.[14]

There are no accusations of vengeance in 1920 as there were in 1901; Freud takes the girl's lack of seriousness and her attempt to manipulate him in perfect stride; he does not give the impression this time that he has been conjuring "up the most evil of those half-tamed demons that inhabit the human breast" (*Dora*, p. 109).

Both of these subject areas—the influence of sexist assumptions on the Freud-Dora relationship and the influence of Dora's sexist milieu on her—can be approached from within the case with the advantage, thereby, of addressing individual factors and reactions. Indeed, our treatment of the transference and countertransference relationships, based on our interpretation of Dora's second dream, explained very fully why Freud treated Dora the way he did and what she thought of it. That entire analysis could be taken as a substantiation of several important points in the feminist critique of Freud. In a parallel manner, we may now turn to the topics of Dora's mother and Dora's love for Frau K.; by examining their importance in the details of the case history, we will see a second intersection of feminist generalizations and individual experience, and Dora's first dream will offer us a crucial clue as to how the general issues became individual ones, how this particular "geography of sex" was incarnated in this particular woman's secrets.

Dora's Loves

Dora began the session in which she told her first dream with an odd gesture: "As I came into the room in which she was waiting she hurriedly concealed a letter which she was reading. I naturally asked her whom the letter was from, and at first she refused to tell me. Something then came out which was a matter of complete indifference and had no relation to the treatment. It was a letter from her grandmother, in which she begged Dora to write to her more often. I believe that Dora only wanted to play 'secrets' with me, and to hint that she was on the point of allowing her secret to be torn from her by the doctor" (*Dora*, p. 78). The dream itself interrupted a discussion which Freud regarded as important; Dora told it "just at a moment when there was a prospect that the material that was coming up for analysis would throw light upon an obscure point in Dora's childhood," he says and, later, "when Dora reported the dream, we were engaged upon a line of enquiry which led straight towards an admission that she had masturbated in childhood" (*Dora*, pp. 64, 74–75). It seems that Dora may have been hiding one secret by offering another, and it may also be true that her attitude towards both secrets was ambivalent, and that she was concealing and indirectly revealing them at the same time.

The letter, naturally, is a more helpful symbol than Freud has time to consider here. Dora has received a letter asking her to write letters, and it is not difficult to find a parallel between this equation and the exchange of constructions and revelations in the analysis. Furthermore, we have already come across several other important letters in the case: Dora's suicide letter, discovered by her parents, was one of the factors that brought her to Freud; the significant letter from Frau K. inviting Dora to the lakeside resort was referred to in her second dream by the letter there from Dora's mother; and a letter concerning her cousin's appendicitis was the occasion for Dora's research on the symptoms that she would later experience herself.

When Freud entered the room Dora put away her letter and took out a dream in which she had couched one of her secrets, for the dream poses the question of the importance of Dora's mother, whose role in Dora's history and in her analysis has been almost completely ignored by Freud, as several writers have pointed out.[15] Hannah Decker writes that "Dora's psychoanalysis is remarkable for the paucity of notice Freud gave to Dora's relationship with her mother" and Jerre Collins and others note that "throughout the analysis Freud acts as if the mother were of no consequence in Dora's psychic life."[16] But Maria Ramas emphasizes the influence of Dora's mother on Dora's attitudes towards heterosexuality, an influence consistent with Freud's remarks in "Female Sexuality," quoted above.[17] Furthermore, it is quite clear that in her later life Dora identified strongly with her mother. Felix Deutsch writes, "Many years went by during which Dora's ego continued in dire need of warding off her feelings of guilt. We learn that she tried to achieve it by an identification with her mother who suffered from a 'housewife's psychosis' consisting of obsessional washing and other kinds of excessive cleanliness. Dora resembled her not only physically but also in this respect" and "[Dora's mother] worked herself to death by her never-ending, daily cleaning compulsion—a task which nobody else could fulfil to her satisfaction. Dora followed in her footsteps, but directed the compulsion mainly to her own body."[18]

Dora's identification with her mother might seem surprising given the fact that she never liked the woman. In presenting the background to the case Freud writes, "The relations between the girl and her mother had been unfriendly for years. The daughter looked down on her mother and used to criticize her mercilessly, and she had withdrawn completely from her influence" (*Dora*, p. 20). These relations seem to have been no better at the time of the treatment for "she was on very bad terms with her mother, who was bent upon drawing her into taking a share in the work of the house" (*Dora*, p. 23). Even twentysome years later, in her second interview with Felix Deutsch, Dora complained about "her premenstrual pains and a vaginal discharge after menstruation. Then she talked mainly about her relationship to her mother, of her unhappy childhood because of her mother's exaggerated cleanliness, her annoying washing compulsions, and her lack of affection for her. Mother's only concern had been her own constipation from which the patient herself now suffered."[19]

Thus the dream raises the first of our two topics, but in a rather problematical way, since the dream features Dora's mother in some prominent connections with the lakeside experience. Furthermore, the mother's prominence in the dream leads directly to our second topic, Dora's love for Frau K., for the dream, in effect, replaces Frau K. with Dora's mother just as it replaces Herr K. with her father. The substitution surprised Dora—"I don't in the least know how Mother comes into the dream; she was not with us at L—— at the time"—

and Freud explains it by building his interpretation of the dream on it: Herr K. "gave you a jewel-case; so you are to give him your jewel-case. . . . In this line of thoughts your mother must be replaced by Frau K. . . . So you are ready to give Herr K. what his wife withholds from him" (*Dora*, pp. 69, 70). This interpretation is consistent, of course, with Freud's emphasis on Dora's love for Herr K. as her most powerful motive. But Freud also places a high value on Dora's love for Frau K., both in the footnote dream interpretation and in his discussion of his shortcomings in the treatment in the postcript (*Dora*, pp. 110n–111n, 120n). As Maria Ramas has pointed out, the two factors conflict: "Freud quickly began to discern, in spite of his own formidable resistance, that Ida Bauer's [Dora's] romantic attachment to Herr K., to the extent that she cultivated such an attachment, was fundamentally utilitarian. In fact, in a series of footnotes, Freud undid his entire analysis by suggesting that behind the 'almost limitless series of displacements' that structured Ida Bauer's symptoms and dreams, 'it was possible to divine the operation of a single simple factor'—Ida's 'deep-rooted homosexual love for Frau K.'"[20]

We will need to qualify Ramas's argument in a moment, but for now we can take note of the contradiction she describes. Ramas argues at length that Dora was dominated by her homosexual love for Frau K. rather than by any substantial interest in Herr K. Freud's identification of Dora's love for Herr K. is based, she says, on "an ideological construct developed in defense of a patriarchal phantasy of femininity and female sexuality." But rather than this, she writes, "Ida Bauer's hysteria was exactly what it appeared to be—a repudiation of the meaning of heterosexuality" and "Ida Bauer's hysteria, insofar as it was a wish, sought to preserve preoedipal love for the mother/woman, and retain access to the maternal/female body. . . . Insofar as her hysteria was denial, it was a repudiation not only of the feminine position in the 'primal scene,' but a continual, unsuccessful attempt to repudiate the 'scene' itself and the sadistic meaning of the phallus. It was an attempt to deny patriarchal sexuality, and a protest against postoedipal femininity."[21] Ramas goes on to examine the influence of Dora's mother on her attitudes towards heterosexuality, pointing out that "quite a few times during the course of the analysis Freud noted that Ida Bauer equated heterosexuality with contamination and self-destruction" and she proposes a strongly eroticized relationship between Dora and Frau K. in which both Dora's father and Herr K. served as screens or foils.[22] This view would help to account for Dora's attitudes after the adults' betrayal of her:

> In revealing Ida's "preoccupation" with sex to Herr K, Frau K not only betrayed Ida, but denied the sexual phantasy they had shared together. For it was not Ida alone who was preoccupied with sexual matters and who read Mantegazza, but Ida and Frau K together. Frau K did indeed sacrifice their erotic relationship in order to protect herself and to preserve her relationship with Philip Bauer [Dora's father]. Frau K's actions reiterated with devastating clarity the sexual law of Ida Bauer's culture. Ida's father stood between her and Frau K as the symbolic Father stands between all women.
>
> Yet, in a sense, Ida Bauer was an outlaw. As Freud noted, Frau K was the one person whom Ida spared, while she pursued the others with an almost malignant vindictiveness. In sparing Frau K, Ida spared herself. In this way she denied both her love for Frau K as well as its futility.[23]

Other writers describe the relationship between Dora and Frau K. in slightly different ways or with a different emphasis. Jacques Lacan writes that Dora found in Frau K. "a mystery, the mystery of her femininity" and that Dora's difficulty lay in "accepting herself as an object of desire for the man"—in which lay the secret of her idolization of Frau K., which Lacan compares with her two-hour meditation in front of the Madonna.[24] Erik Erikson, as we have already seen, suggests that Dora "may well have sought in Mrs. K. . . . that *mentor* who helps the young to overcome unstable identifications with the parent of the same sex."[25] Whatever the exact formulation, it is clear that Dora's attachment to Frau K. was a strong one and, by the evidence which exists in the case history, a more powerful factor than her interest in Herr K. Freud suggests as much, as Ramas acknowledges, but mainly in the postscript, after the fact of the analysis. He makes no attempt to resolve the contradiction that Ramas has highlighted—that between Dora's "love" for Frau K. and her "love" for Herr K.—even though that contradiction puts a good portion of his analysis on a precarious footing. Nor are we compelled to accept Ramas's interpretation of homosexual love in its most overtly erotic form in order to recognize the conflict.[26] What must be determined next, however, is the extent to which that contradiction was an element of Dora's experience rather than of Freud's interpretation.

For even if we grant much of Ramas's argument, it does not seem that we can deny that Dora had *any* interest in Herr K. (notice her mention of his postcard in the quotation from Freud which follows). The fact that Freud may be overemphasizing the *importance* of that interest or imposing his own (and his culture's) sexist assumptions in describing the *nature* of the interest does not negate the considerable evidence in Dora's history that attests to it.[27] If Dora had no interest of any kind in Herr K., she must have been the most remarkable hypocrite of the age. We are forced, therefore, to acknowledge Dora's involvement with both Frau and Herr K., even though those relationships seem to conflict.

Thus far we have a related pair of paradoxes. On the one hand, Dora's relationship with her mother seems problematical insofar as we find Dora identifying with the woman she disliked so long and so intensely and whom she had seemed to replace with Frau K. On the other hand, Dora's interests in Frau K. and her husband seem to conflict, for even if we are willing to grant an unusual intensity to Dora's love for Frau K., as Ramas would have it, we cannot ignore altogether the evidence for her interest in Herr K. as well. To put the matter another way, Dora's love for Frau K. may well have been her most powerful interest in these relationships, as Ramas argues and as Freud later came to believe; but that love ran counter to two other relationships, Dora's identification with her mother and her interest in Herr K. This complicated situation becomes a little clearer in the description of it that Kurt Schlesinger has formulated:

> Dora's feelings about Mrs. K. as an intimate, a confidante, a sexual mentor, a person on whom she had a crush, were in oppositional tension with those in which she felt drawn to Mr. K. and her father.
> In earlier years while wanting her father, Dora could not tolerate these wishes and repressed them. They returned in a compromise form of symptoms wherein both wish and countervailing notions are contained. With this unresolved conflict and its symptomatic forms she subsequently deals ambivalently, and she finally overtly rejects Mr. K. who, among other aspects, is a father surrogate.
> She has responded to the verbal seduction of Mrs. K., the mother surrogate, developed a crush on her which may in part reinforce her capacity to reject Mr. K. In a contradictory fashion, the motivation for retaining her closeness to Mrs. K. may be in order to—or not to—get that close to Mr. K., via his wife.
> Thus, also with father, she wants him for herself and begrudges Mrs. K.'s closeness to him. She wants Mrs. K. for herself and feels rivalrous with her father. In a complex layering kind of way, each of her involvements is ambivalently cathected, and she can use the other two relationships to safeguard against the full recognition of her feelings in any one of them.[28]

Schlesinger's description exposes the precarious, ambivalent web of Dora's attachments before the lakeside scene and suggests how that emotional network contained some of the seeds of its own undoing, given the occasion of Herr K.'s proposition. We should supplement this description by adding some of our earlier observations: after Dora rejected Herr K., she "returned" to her mother as well as to her father. Once the accusations had been made against her, she withdrew exclusively towards her mother, though without liking her any better than she had, it seems. In other words, the comprehensive and precarious pattern which Schlesinger describes was entirely destroyed by the lakeside incident. Dora's love for Frau K. may have helped her reject Herr K., but she also lost both Frau K. and her father by the time she was done.

Having gotten this far, we can shift the terms of our question a bit. There is no great difficulty in understanding Dora's identification with her mother if it is placed chronologically. That identification became pre-eminent only after Dora lost her ties to the other three adults. The question now becomes, why did Dora allow those connections to be broken? In the previous chapters we discussed the effect of the adults' betrayal on her, and none of that should be forgotten. But that conspiracy was not the beginning of things here; it was, in fact, a defensive reaction to Dora's accusation of Herr K. In other words, Dora was partly responsible for destroying her own network of relationships, not by refusing Herr K. but by exposing him in a way that forced the adults to react. Granted that their reaction took a form which Dora probably did not expect; but what, then, *did* she expect? Why did Dora tell her mother about Herr K.'s proposition?

On the face of it, the answer may seem obvious; if Herr K.'s proposition was as insulting and traumatic as the preceding analysis has claimed, then naturally Dora would turn to her parents for help. If she was as angry at and disappointed in Herr K. as Freud believes, then revealing his improper behavior would be likely revenge. But as natural or obvious as this action might have been in another situation, it was not in Dora's. During the analysis she herself was puzzled by the action (*Dora*, p. 95). The very intricacy of her relationships with the three adults and her ambivalent attitude towards Herr K. in particular complicate the matter. Furthermore, this is the same girl who did not report Herr K.'s earlier affront and who continued to receive gifts from him and to share his company after that episode, who countenanced and implicitly supported her father's affair with Frau K., and who had made herself knowledgeable in sexual matters under Frau K.'s tutelage. Lacan notes that her father's affair was maintained "not only on the basis of her silence, but through the complicity of Dora herself, and, what is more, even under her vigilant protection."²⁹ In addition to those factors, Dora must surely have realized that her action would have repercussions beyond its effect on Herr K. How did she expect Frau K. to react, both to the fact of the proposition and to Dora's decision to reveal it? Presumably Dora expected her father to take precisely the action he did—at first—that is, to call Herr K. to a formal accounting. Did she expect Frau K. to join in a chorus of indignation, or to stand silently aside, discreetly sympathetic? And what effect, for that matter, was Dora's action likely to have on the arrangement between her father and Frau K., which depended, in some degree, on the begrudging acquiescence of Herr K.? Freud remarks at one point that Dora's father

> was one of those men who know how to evade a dilemma by falsifying their judgement upon one of the conflicting alternatives. If it had been pointed out to him that there might be danger for a growing girl in the constant and unsupervised companionship of a man who had no satisfaction from his own wife, he would have been certain to answer that he could rely upon his daughter, that a man like K. could never be dangerous to her, and that his friend was himself incapable of such intentions, or that Dora was still a child and was treated as a child by K. But as a matter of fact things were in a position in which each of the two men avoided drawing any conclusions from the other's behaviour which would have been awkward for his own plans. (*Dora*, pp. 34–35)

Had Dora no conception at all, after almost ten years of the arrangement, of the thin tissue of hypocrisy behind which it thrived or of the awkwardness of the public reverberations of her charge?

The fact is that Dora's action was bound to disrupt the intrigue in some way, beyond its effects on Herr K. himself. Schlesinger makes clear Dora's considerable investment in these arrangements; yet in telling her mother about Herr K. she put them all at hazard. Nor is it believable that her desire for revenge on Herr K. outweighed the whole emotional construction—or, indeed, *either* of the other two relationships involved. We are brought to ask, therefore, what possible motive of Dora's could have been stronger than these earlier attachments. What was so important to her then that it made her either headstrong or careless about all the relationships that, until then, had been more important than anything else?

The radical nature of Dora's action is more apparent in another detail: it was not her parents she told, but her mother. Can we assume, knowing what we do about Dora's attitude towards her mother on the one hand, and about her adoration of Frau K. (her mother surrogate) on the other, that she merely took the normal recourse of an adolescent girl in a difficult situation? Freud states that Dora intended "that what she said should be passed on to her father" (*Dora*, p. 25), a more than likely surmise. Why, then, did she not tell her father? Or Frau K., who had been thoroughly frank with her about her opinion of her husband ("She had been the wife's confidante and adviser in all the difficulties of her married life. There was nothing they had not talked about" [*Dora*, p. 61])? We are brought back to the same question: what motive of Dora's suddenly became more compelling than all her relationships?

At various times during the analysis Freud identifies three different reproaches of Dora's strong enough to be considered possible motives. Two of them, however, came too late to explain Dora's decision to expose Herr K. First, after the lakeside scene Dora became obsessed with her father's affair and tried to get him to end it;[30] second, Dora was outraged at the accusation that she had merely imagined the proposition. While both of these motives were very strong, they were both reactions to the conspiracy of the adults, not to the proposition itself.

There was a third complaint, however, which directly supported both of these and which might have been working earlier, and that was the idea that Dora had been bartered. Freud tells us, "When she was feeling embittered she used to be overcome by the idea that she had been handed over to Herr K. as the price of his tolerating the relations between her father and his wife; and her rage at her father's making such a use of her was visible behind her affection for him" (*Dora*, p. 34). Naturally this realization was dramatically enforced by the adults' conspiracy, but there is no reason that it could not have occurred to Dora earlier than that; Dora might have realized the terms of the barter before she decided to expose Herr K. In fact, his proposition could have sparked the insight. When he told her that he "got nothing from his wife," Dora knew the reason as well as he, and perhaps she could not help but finish the thought: "... therefore, I will get something from you; you are the exchange." Dora's knowledge of the young governess's fate gave the proposition a very specific implication in Dora's eyes. If Herr K. saw no more in her than a temporary mistress and if her father and Frau K. would tolerate this use of Dora for the sake of the exchange, then... Perhaps the realization dawned on Dora while Herr K. was speaking to her, or shortly after that; at any rate, Dora's sudden understanding of her position in the sexual economy of the adults would better explain the traumatic value of Herr K.'s proposition and Dora's willingness, in exposing him, to risk upsetting her longstanding arrangement with all three characters. To her horror, the arrangement suddenly seemed much different from what she had supposed it to be. She had long ago lost her father to Frau K. but she had accommodated herself to that development by implicitly supporting their affair and by her intimate relationship with Frau K. herself.[31] She had not realized, before Herr K.'s proposition, the extent to which she had lost Frau K. to her father. It was because she saw herself as a bartered object that Dora began attacking the liaison she had formerly implicitly supported; the united accusation of the adults confirmed her insight in the most vivid way possible.[32]

This puts a rather different light on Dora's decision to tell her mother about Herr K. If, in fact, she recognized the barter before reporting him, sometime in the two weeks between his proposition and her exposure of it, then her decision to tell her mother can only have been a destructive act aimed, not only at Herr K., but at Frau K. and her father as well. Dora acted out of a sense of outrage, a consequent desire for revenge on all three adults, and, likely enough, a feeling of hopelessness at the realization which "overwhelmed" her. At the same time, her action may have been a more or less desperate test of loyalty: she would see how her father and Frau K. responded to the disruption she was causing and whether their reactions confirmed or contradicted her disturbing realization.

This interpretation, suggested by the circumstances we have been considering, is supported by Dora's first dream in which Frau K. is replaced by Dora's mother.[33] In effect, Dora retreats from her intimacy with Frau K., whom she "adored," to a preoedipal identification with her mother, whom she despised, and so this dream prefigures the mother's role in the second dream as well as Dora's later identification with her. It is the timing which is significant here. Both dreams rejected Frau K., but the first dream did so before Dora reported Herr K.'s proposition. In the two weeks following that dream Dora became convinced that all three adults had bartered her and that Frau K., like the earlier governess, had been interested in her only because of her father.

Dora's Choice

Thinking again of our earlier distinction between external and internal factors in terms of these more recent considerations, we might be tempted to draw the lines somewhat differently. The proposition Herr K. made to Dora embodied sexist assumptions which are clear enough, and Dora, thanks to the warning example of the young governess, read them for what they were.[34] The proposition demanded of Dora a sexual maturity which she did not yet possess because she was unwilling to abandon her childish attachments to Frau K., to her father, and even to Herr K. himself. More than that, however, the proposition offered Dora a sexual role she could not accept, the demeaning position of a "sexual governess." This was heterosexuality of a very particular kind. Dora's recognition of it for what it was, though, led her to the traumatic realization that she had, in effect, already been cast in just such a role by all the adults on whose love she relied. Dora's evaluation of the sexist assumptions of the adults, that is, led her to an understanding of her own situation and options.

If she could not accept Herr K.'s offer, then she must also refuse her father's and Frau K.'s, once she had seen through them, for the role of a sexual pawn was no better than that of a governess.

This development led Dora to another insight, to a further understanding of the range of options available to her as a woman, best seen in the self-portrait in her second dream. The further insight was even more comprehensive and more distressing than its predecessors. It was, in fact, the most disheartening aspect of Dora's situation, for it showed the degree to which the sexist assumptions of her milieu were also her own. The final insight was that, having rejected the demeaning roles offered her by the adults, she could imagine no other options. She had seen through the hypocrisy of the parts they played in their well-established intrigue, and she had seen through the hypocrisy behind the part they offered her—at no small cost to her sense of self. But having rejected those roles, Dora could conceive of no other for herself; she could conceive of herself, that is, in no other terms. She might reject the past indignantly, but she was unable to construct a future. As the bleak determination of her second dream shows, her only option was to reject.

Chapter Six

Implications

The Significance of the Case

In Freud's first case history both he and his patient said more than they meant to. Freud was determined to use the material of the case to illustrate his theory of the interpretation of dreams, to show the strategic value of dreams in analysis, and to demonstrate his theory of hysterical symptom formation. The form of the case history allowed him to do here what he was not able to do in *The Interpretation of Dreams* and what needed to be done in order to substantiate and illustrate his theory of dream interpretation: the case history allowed Freud to investigate both symptom and dream in thorough detail. His theory was, in important respects, a theory of details, but the limitations he naturally imposed on the illustrations in *The Interpretation of Dreams*—in the awkward circumstance that the most detailed analytical material available to him was that of his self-analysis, he understandably curtailed his exposition of sensitive personal matter—prevented him from offering even a single demonstration of his theory, a single example which traced the latent content of a dream all the way back to its remote unconscious sources.[1] He was forced, in his great book, to settle for a catalogue of partial illustrations, none of which put his theory to an exhaustive test. How could he convince his readers that an infantile, unconscious wish lay behind every dream unless he could show that it lay behind at least one? Not only that, but he must also show the trail of discovery, the path of investigation which, according to his theory, led from the dream back to its ultimate "meaning." And finally, he must show that both the latent meaning and the method by which it could be discovered justified his strategic analogy between dreams and symptoms. For all of these purposes he needed a case history, an "objective" illustration full of the wealth of detail necessary to present a comprehensive demonstration; and the case history must be one in which dreams occupied a commanding position in that wealth of material. Dora's case was perfectly suited to these needs in spite of its unsatisfactory conclusion. The material of Dora's analysis could illustrate the discovery of the mechanism of the symptom, if not its cure, and the unravelling of the hidden meaning of the dream, if not its therapeutic manipulation.

Freud was right in thinking that his theoretical argument required this sort of illustration, and he was right to choose an example which could be explored so thoroughly, in which the bewildering variety and complexity of specifics could be taken account of and organized. In no other way could he convincingly validate the large claims he had made in his theoretical book, for the large claims depended on a plethora of hidden details. The large claims themselves were crucial, as Freud knew very well. His theory of dreams was already more than a theory of dreams. Freud's whole concept of human psychology was at stake because he had chosen to expound it in terms of the dream, his "royal road to the unconscious." It was his dream theory which made the world of the unconscious largely accessible to him and largely explainable to his readers. Almost everything else followed from that.

The "Fragment of an Analysis of a Case of Hysteria," therefore, was an extremely important piece of work for Freud; it still occupies a unique position and carries an exclusive authority among all the works of his twenty-three volumes. Nowhere else does Freud offer both the evidence and the details of his methodology for such close scrutiny in the interpretation of a complicated dream. It is here and only here that Freud's theory and practice of dream interpretation can be examined in depth.

But when the dreams in the case history are examined, there is more than meets the eye. It is true, as Freud claims, that the two dreams dominate and synthesize the material, the convoluted trails of memories, associations, and facts in which Dora was entangled. The dreams do open the door to Dora's psyche and history; they present and explain something of her symptoms, and they offer a rich test of Freud's theories. The results, however, are not what Freud would have predicted, and the aptness of the case for my purpose lies not only in its strategic importance in Freud's work, but in the way in which the apparent difficulties—the troubled transference and countertransference relationships and the abrupt termination—reflect and verify a more fundamental strain. The dreams do not behave entirely as they are supposed to, and although they serve Freud well in starting lines of inquiry which help clarify the symptoms and their histories, it almost seems that he is using the wrong end of the hammer. The dreams tell more than he realized, more than his theory allows them to tell. What is unusual about the function of the dreams and their interpretation in this case—in addition to the wealth of detail—is that the discord between the Freudian interpretation of the dreams and the dreams themselves reverberates into the analysis and illuminates, perhaps contributes to, the discord in the doctor-patient relationship. Simply because of the terms and conditions of the analysis, and especially because it was terminated so abruptly, Freud did not have the opportunity to take the long way around, to circumnavigate the difficulties which arose. Later, more adept at assessing and manipulating the transference relationship, he might well have survived the disturbance or even have avoided the worst of it. In this case, however, he was not able to escape the storm because the dreams on which he relied so heavily performed in ways his theory could not take account of, and he had no time for alternate procedures.

That, then, is the point of my reexamination of Dora's analysis: the dreams do not conform to Freud's theory, and the outcome of the analysis helps to illustrate that point. The dreams are coherent and, when read for their coherence, throw an entirely different light on the material of the case. Freud's theory dictated that the dreams be treated as *not* coherent, that they should be regarded as jumbles of likely clues, disorganized assortments of pregnant hints which, followed up individually, would eventually lead to material worth examination in its own right. Freud's failure to notice even the most obvious formal characteristics of the second dream is a good indication of the degree to which he refused to consider the possibility of manifest coherence. Even had he been open to that possibility, he lacked the analytic tools required, as he demonstrated elsewhere, particularly in his studies of Leonardo Da Vinci and of Michelangelo's *Moses*. Dreams are coherent in a particular way and respond to a particular kind of analysis.

It is true, of course, that hints of something miscarried or incomplete are quite clear at several points in the case history. Freud speculates on the difficulty with his usual frankness, if not his usual acuity. He is right to the point, at least, of fixing on the transference relationship as the nub of the problem. But his reasoning on this topic is weak and unconvincing, as we have seen, even several years after the analysis—assuming that most of the postscript was composed nearer the publication date of 1905 than his first writing up of the history in January 1901. And, of course, Freud entirely overlooks the matter of the countertransference.

That topic has been dealt with by a number of commentators though it is puzzling that, until recently, so little attention had been paid to the unusual situation—unusual in the whole corpus of Freud's work. The consensus among those who have reevaluated the case is that Freud was unaware of a countertransference from himself to Dora (in the role of Herr K., primarily) which biased several of his reactions and reflections. We have offered further details in support of this interpretation in the course of examining the implications of Dora's second dream. But the dream—read aesthetically—offers an entirely new insight which not only complements this one but, in combination with it, explains very clearly exactly why Dora terminated her analysis. It is quite possible to construct a reasonable hypothesis about the countertransference without such reference to the details of the dreams in the case, *but only Dora's dreams, and particularly the second, clarify the transference from Dora to Freud.* Freud's assumption, generally accepted by later students of the case, was that Dora saw him in terms of Herr K. and transferred to him on that basis. Somewhere behind the figure of Herr K. in this transference stood that of her father. But this understanding of Dora's attitude, especially in the final weeks of the analysis, was itself part of Freud's difficulty with the countertransference, and this interpretation tells us more about Freud's stance than it does about Dora's. Because Freud cast himself in the role of Herr K., he thought that Dora also saw him in that role (even though he was apparently unaware that he had so cast himself). It is only from her second dream that we can discover otherwise. The dream tells us that Dora's transference to Freud at that point in the analysis was based on her attitudes towards her father, not towards Herr K. Not only does our aesthetic reading of the second dream propose this new understanding of Dora's transference, but it also sketches the reason that her transference took this form and its implications in the analysis. The chief implication was, of course, her decision to terminate. If we combine our understanding of Freud's stance with this new interpretation of Dora's, we can see very clearly what Dora's motive was when she left. There was, as we might call it, a collision of illusions towards the end of the analysis. Freud not only adopted Herr K.'s role, he assumed that Dora saw him in that role. But Dora saw him primarily in terms of her father, not Herr K., and, ironically, Freud's enactment of the role of Herr K. only confirmed Dora's view of him as a new version of her father, the father who was the original object of her love and who was, therefore, capable of the most comprehensive betrayal of her. To Dora, Freud became her betraying father. The mutual misunderstanding between Dora and Freud matched perfectly. Dora looked to Freud for one father and found another: she found the father who betrayed her by adopting Herr K.'s viewpoint just when she had turned to him for protection from Herr K. In this light, Dora's decision to leave and even the curt way in which she acted out that decision make perfect, if unfortunate, sense.

Dora's second dream, therefore, is coherent to a purpose. A careful reading of that dream provides more information about the dynamics of the case than is otherwise available; it coordinates and synthesizes much of the information that Freud recovered in the analysis and offers a final "statement" which explains, in a thorough and convincing way, those dynamics of the analysis that were responsible for its outcome.

Freud's Manifest Practice

It would be well to stand back from the details of the case history and those of our own analysis in order to suggest some of the implications of this work. If the foregoing analysis demonstrates that a dream can be coherent at the manifest level, what does that imply about Freud's theory of dreams?

The opportunities of this particular example have allowed a more thorough and concrete demonstration than might have been possible otherwise. Precisely because Freud's interpretation is incomplete and at odds with some of the facts of the case, the contrast between his method and an aesthetic interpretation is sharper. But the validity of the hypothesis of aesthetic coherence does not depend on the failure of a psychoanalytic construction. The relationship between the two methodologies is far more complex and problematical than it might first appear, and in other situations the comparison might take on quite a different coloring. Freud's analysis of Dora's first dream, for example, shows a much closer relationship with a reading of the dream's aesthetically constructed surface. There, the main features of his interpretation conform quite closely to the manifest details of the dream.[2] The short dream is composed of a setting ("a house"), a plot conflict (escaping from the fire), a few characters (Dora and her family), and a few key symbols (the house, the fire, the jewel case). In the surface narrative of the dream, Dora's father helps her escape from the danger of the fire in spite of her mother's opposing interests. Obviously these elements are integrated and coherent on the manifest level—the dream reads like a very short story or a scene in a story—and Freud's interpretation utilizes this coherence. So, for example, the fire symbolizes the danger of passion; in the dream narrative Dora's father helps her escape from the fire in the house; in Freud's interpretation Dora turns to her father to escape from the danger of her passion for Herr K. The elements that are related in the surface narrative in a literal way are similarly related in the pattern of Freud's interpretation. In fact, Freud's reading *depends upon* the dream's literal coherence since he does not find it necessary to establish separate or alternate connections among these elements or among the latent references of these elements. If the dream were not already coherent at the manifest level, Freud's interpretation of it would make no sense.[3]

There is some support for a similar conclusion—that a psychoanalytic interpretation is most cogent and pertinent when it aligns itself with the internal coherence of the manifest dream—in Freud's treatment of Dora's second dream, although that situation is much more complex. Freud's theory of interpretation flatly opposes this sort of strategy, of course; according to it the analyst should, under no circumstances, consider manifest coherence. In fact, if a dream appears to be coherent, that in itself is grounds for heightened suspicion of its manifest form.[4] The analyst must fragment the dream as he finds it and treat each of the fragments in isolation, pressing though the matrix of associated materials until he arrives at the latent meaning of the dream. He must not look back over his shoulder at the manifest dream which serves, in his view, merely as a jumbled collection of clues and starting points. Once he has found the latent meaning, he has no reason to return to the manifest dream since it was only the latent meaning which interested him in the first place. The method is clear in theory and Freud often adheres to it, but he also frequently violates it in the course of a detailed interpretation such as this one.

In fact, if we look back over Freud's analysis of Dora's second dream, we see that, in reality, he treats the manifest level of the dream in three distinctly different ways. His most frequent practice is to ignore surface congruities altogether, in accordance with his own theory. Examples of this practice are very frequent in his analysis of

Dora's second dream; most of the harmonies and relationships among specific elements that we considered in chapter 2, "The Art of Dora's Dream," have no place at all in Freud's analysis. He simply is not interested in structural forms or thematic continuity or patterns of imagery. But once we have observed these devices and the degree to which they build harmonies into the dream, we must conclude that the dream commands an entire dimension that Freud has bypassed.

In other instances, however, Freud completely contravenes existing surface harmonies, most often by separating elements that are linked in the manifest text or by linking elements that the manifest dream distinguishes from one another. This, too, we would expect as a consequence of his theory and method, and this category of examples is really only a subset of the previous category; that is, Freud contradicts surface harmonies precisely because he is ignoring them. Nonetheless, these examples are worth isolating because of the interesting questions they pose: they seem to juxtapose the two interpretive methods, literary and psychoanalytic, most pointedly and thus raise the question of their relationship very clearly. In the examples that can be drawn from the analysis of Dora's second dream the juxtaposition is especially suggestive since Freud's interpretation seems to miss the mark or fall short most often when this conflict occurs. When he ignores surface patterns in this dream, his reading becomes oblique or obscure; when he contradicts those surface patterns, however, his readings become positively misleading. Thus we saw that his conflation of the three distinct dream scenes into a single "geography of sex" and his concomitant treatment of the symbols in those scenes as virtual equivalents led him to a distorted view of Dora's role in the dream. Our criticism must be, finally, not that there is no "geography of sex" in the dream, but that Freud's version of it is simplified, levelled, and fails to acknowledge the variety and complexity of that geography and of Dora's progression through it. Freud's reading here is reductive in the worst sense, and the effects of this strategy are all too apparent in the outcome of the case.

An alternate example of the same phenomenon is the instance in which Freud's interpretation contradicts the dream by ignoring harmonies that exist in it, by treating distinct elements as entirely unrelated even though the dream has related them. Here the results can be equally damaging. Freud has little to say, for example, about the man in the woods, the dream character who refers most directly to him. He entirely overlooks that character's appearance in a sequence of characters or character roles (Dora's absent father; the man in the woods; Dora's buried father), his pivotal position in the plot of the dream, and the structural positioning of his appearance at dead center of the middle section and therefore also of the dream as a whole. It is these relationships between the character and the other elements in the dream, including the other characters, that not only suggest Freud's symbolic role but also define that role in relation to Dora's father, thus controlling the whole transference reference of the dream. Because the man in the woods is juxtaposed against Dora's father, we understand that Dora's reaction to Freud can be juxtaposed against her reaction to her father.

These examples and the others we could select from the analysis in the preceding four chapters all bring us to the same point: the dream is aesthetically constructed; to ignore its aesthetic mechanisms is to ignore its meaning. A given element "A" and another element "B" in the dream not only cohere and establish meaning by means of that coherence (i.e., the relationship between them contributes to the meaning of the dream), but the individual meanings of the separate elements are also controlled by their relationships. Individual elements mutually confer and influence their individual significances. It is no wonder that withdrawing them from their contextual network and treating them as isolated clues leads, as it so often does for Freud, to a welter of further subjects and lines of inquiry, the associated material which is not the dream and which, frequently enough, leads nowhere in particular beyond itself. By definition, it always leads away from the dream.

Freud does not always adhere to his own theory, though, and his third method of handling manifest elements, unlike the first two we have noted, directly violates his proscription against considering coherence at the manifest level. In these instances Freud relies upon relationships in the manifest text and silently uses them in his search for latent meaning. That he does so gives strong warrant to a theory of manifest coherence and raises questions about the relationship between the manifest text and Freudian latent meaning—questions which indicate a far more complicated state of affairs than even Freud supposes. In short, the theoretical implications of these few examples are very broad.

Freud's implicit use of manifest harmonies is apparent in several places. Perhaps the most obvious of these is the connection he makes between the death of Dora's father, announced early in the dream, and Dora's last act in the dream—"she went calmly [*or*, not the least sadly] to her room, and began reading a big book that lay on her writing table" (*Dora*, p. 100). Freud connects the big book with an encyclopedia, in which Dora might have read about forbidden subjects, through an indirect trail of memories, fantasies, and symptoms. When the implications of reading the big book are finally developed, the relationship between these two manifest elements becomes clear:

> The emphasis here was upon the two details "calmly" and "big" in connection with "book." I asked whether the book was in encyclopaedia *format*, and she said it was. Now children never read about forbidden subjects in an encyclopaedia *calmly*. They do it in fear and trembling, with an uneasy look over their shoulder to see if some one may not be coming. Parents are very much in the way while reading of this kind is going on. But this uncomfortable situation had been radically improved, thanks to the dream's power of fulfilling wishes. Dora's father was dead, and the others had already gone to the cemetery. She might calmly read whatever she chose. Did not this mean that one of her motives for revenge was a revolt against her parents' constraint? If her father was dead she could read or love as she pleased.   (*Dora*, p. 100)

Here Freud has made the manifest connection by means of a series of associations and latent connections. Two elements in the dream, the father's death and the big book, are shown to be directly and significantly related to each other. Freud uses the manifest connection (he explains the book in terms of its relation to the death of Dora's father) but he does not acknowledge it as a manifest connection, nor does he in any way distinguish it from the links he makes among the associations and latent dream-thoughts. In fact, the manifest connection is more intricate than Freud realizes. In the dream, Dora may read now that her father is dead. But her father's death is announced to her in a letter, which she also reads. Furthermore, she reads the big book that lay on her writing table, where she might write letters herself. These two elements of the manifest dream—her father's death announced at the beginning and her own reading at the end—are thus related by ironically parallel imagery as well as by simple causality in the plot. These additional connections are not gratuitous; if the book is understood in relation to Mantegazza's *Physiology of Love* and if the death of Dora's father is understood as part of her reaction to his betrayal of her, then the dream has only reinforced its central theme by making these connections between the two elements. The stylistic device is more than a technicality.

Thus far we can see that the two manifest images share relations in the latent dream thoughts as well as relations on a purely manifest level. They are also joined by a kind of mixed relation, or mixed combinations of manifest and latent connections which serve as additional bridges. In this example, the mixed relations form a third bond between the two images. The act of reading the big book is connected to the death of Dora's father via the manifest image of Dora's climbing the stairs to the room where she reads the book, an action which suggests Dora's earlier symptom of dragging her foot. This symptom in turn suggests the case of appendicitis (or false pregnancy) which occurred nine months after the seduction scene at the lake and which was associated with an accident in which she twisted her foot while going downstairs, at the age of eight, shortly before her attack of nervous asthma, a symptom related to her masturbation, her perception of her parents' sexual activity, and her love for her father, especially during an absence (*Dora*, pp. 79–82, 100–104). Thus, through an involved chain of symptoms and fantasies, the death (absence) of Dora's father is related to Dora's reading of the big book by means of a third manifest image, that of her climbing the stairs. The connection by this route, as even a summary of Freud's analysis shows, is complicated and oblique. The point remains, however, that Freud has constructed a chain of connections in which both latent and manifest elements function, and the final connection, made with the help of latent elements, is one between two manifest elements in the dream. Needless to say, both the procedure and the result are very different in nature from anything that Freud's theory of interpretation describes.

As we might suspect, other examples of this phenomenon abound in Freud's demonstrations of dream analysis, in *The Interpretation of Dreams* as well as here. In the simplest terms, Freudian theory categorically denies and therefore refuses to explore a phenomenon—manifest coherence—which Freud frequently illustrates in practice. If Freud says that the manifest dream is *not* coherent, but repeatedly demonstrates that it *is* coherent, what are we to make of his theory of dreams? In other words, what lines of inquiry are suggested by the hypotheses of manifest coherence?

Finding the Text

Perhaps we should preface a very brief sketch of the implications of this analysis of Dora's dream by acknowledging, on the one hand, the limitations of any single example, no matter how strategic, and by claiming, on the other hand, that Dora's dream is *essentially* representative of the phenomenon, notwithstanding certain differences of degree in some of its qualities and certain unusual circumstances of its original context.

One might argue that Dora's dreams are coherent but are unusual in that respect and that the example we have chosen would turn out to be an elaborate exception in a more broadly based investigation. It is true that some of the circumstances of the reporting of the dream ought to be noted. Freud remarks on Dora's intelligence, for example, and it is clear from the case history as well as from our interpretation of it that she was less than cooperative and tried, especially near the end of the analysis, to manipulate Freud and the analytic situation, for reasons that we discovered in the previous two chapters. It is conceivable that her intelligence or her attitude towards the analysis influenced the form of the dream as she told it to Freud. Or again, Freud is rather vague on the timing of the dreams; the first dream was one that Dora had had "a few nights earlier" (*Dora*, p. 64) than the session in which she reported it, and although the second dream seems to have been reported the day after its occurrence (*Dora*, pp. 97–98), Freud does not situate all the addenda to the dream exactly (none of which is trivial), so that we cannot know precisely when they occurred to Dora, in what order, or how they were related to (or suggested by) the topics of discussion in the sessions.[5] We might remember, too, that the texts which Freud gives us have gone through the additional process of his memory; after commenting on the difficulty of retrieving material without having taken notes during a session, Freud at one point explains that the "wording of these dreams was recorded immediately after the session," and he concludes, about the case material as a whole, that "the record is not absolutely—phonographically—exact, but it can claim to possess a high degree of trustworthiness. Nothing of any importance has been altered in it except in some places the order in which the explanations are given; and this has been done for the sake of presenting the case in a more connected form" (*Dora*, pp. 9–10). Freud's comment raises an unavoidable question about the fidelity of the texts of the dreams that he prints, especially for an analysis such as the foregoing one which relies heavily on precise details.

In view of these considerations we must allow the possibility that the texts of Dora's dreams may be, somehow or to some degree, less authentic than we would wish. And each of these considerations raises theoretical questions well worth pursuing in their own right. But these qualifications do not affect the validity of the analysis we have been conducting in the previous chapters for the simple reason that these factors, if indeed they have been operative, would have made the dream less coherent or less pertinent to its analytic context, or both. The question of Dora's intelligence, for example, is a red herring. If we were to allow ourselves to suppose that her dreams are more coherent than some others because she is more intelligent than some other dreamers, we would be faced with the suggestion that only some dreams are unified and that intelligence is a contributing factor. This would complicate an investigation of the hypotheses of aesthetic coherence, but would not disqualify it. In this situation, we would still need to account for the unity of "intelligent" dreams and, as far as they would be concerned, the terrain of the inquiry would not change a whit. We would have the added topic of "unintelligent" dreams, though, and would need to explain the factors that made them so, the difference between them and their more ordered counterparts. Freudian theory is not prepared to deal with either of these categories, or with any form of the question of aesthetic coherence or its absence. Our two hypotheses could at least address the one category and distinguish it from the second.

In point of fact, however, there is no indication that Dora's dreams are any more intelligent than most others, however astute she may have been. Studies of large numbers of "average" dreams habitually report narrative coherence and organization and the presence of fictionlike qualities. Dreams collected in sleep laboratories or gathered under less rigidly controlled conditions for content analysis may be less interesting and less intricate, in the main, than Dora's dreams, but they are no closer to Freud's description of what a dream should be than hers are. The differences are differences of degree and style. We should realize, too, that it is unfair to compare the dream that has been extensively analysed, as this one has, to those that have not; naturally Dora's dream looks unusually sophisticated because we have taken unusual pains with it. The aesthetic qualities we are ascribing to this and other dreams are not always immediately apparent, or there would be no point to this sort of analysis in the first place. Another consideration is that Dora's dreams occurred at critical points in her rather complicated life and that the available subject matter for her at this particular time was itself both intricate and emotionally charged. Other dreams may not always have the advantage of such raw material and so may turn out to be as literary in their devices and structures as they are mundane in their subject matter.

The possibility that Dora may have consciously or unconsciously adjusted the texts of her dreams in order to render them more suitable instruments for manipulating Freud and the analytic situation is a problematic topic. It is a commonplace that dreams often respond to their contexts, therapeutic or otherwise; it has been noted that analysands of Freudians show a remarkable preference for Freudian-style dreams while Jungian patients conveniently adopt a more appropriate Jungian style. Naturally it is sometimes difficult to sort out the dream from its telling and its interpretation in making these comparisons. Some studies have addressed noticeable differences between dreams recorded in sleep laboratories and those recorded at home, however, so that it seems that dreams are quite willing to respond to topical emphases and interpretative methodologies in choosing their own idioms.

This variety of potential styles in no way compromises the hypotheses of aesthetic coherence, for it is characteristic of aesthetic compositions that they avail themselves of just this kind of flexibility. Within a large universe of available devices, combinations, and structures, a given composition features a relatively limited specific range.

The question of a tendentious revision remains more difficult, however. The argument here would have to run something like this: in order to serve some ulterior motive, Dora unconsciously rendered her dreams less dreamlike and more aesthetic. Assuming, for the moment, that aesthetic qualities are less dreamlike, we are left with the question of what ulterior motive might be served by such a revision. It does not seem likely that such a revision would be at all responsive to Dora's analytic situation, however, since Freud was paying no attention to aesthetic factors. Perhaps, on the other hand, such a revision would have served as a method of resistance by which Dora could frustrate Freud's attempts at analysis. In one sense, of course, the aesthetic nature of these two dreams did frustrate Freud's efforts, though there is nothing peculiar about Dora's case in that respect: Freud was categorically immune to aesthetic considerations, as we have already noted. But the real point here is that the aesthetic mode of the dreams in no way served Dora's interests; rather, it was Freud's failure to recognize and respond to the content of the dreams, aesthetically constructed as they were, which aggravated Dora's dissatisfaction. If Dora was unconsciously revising her dreams in order to make them obscure, the chaotic manifest form that Freud describes would have been more effective or, if they were to be coherent, they should have been coherent on indifferent or deceptive topics.

Much of the same argument could be applied to the charge that the dreams are not safe examples because of a large measure of secondary revision. It is quite possible that both of Dora's dreams were subjected to a significant degree to this device of the Freudian dream-work that revises the "original" dream in order to make it appear more coherent. Freud's usual reaction to the kind of orderliness we have found in Dora's second dream— had he taken account of it— would certainly have been to suspect a heavy degree of secondary revision. Perhaps, therefore, the texts of Dora's dreams are more coherent than the original dreams were. According to Freud's description of this device of the dream-work, the original dream is tidied up at the manifest level in order to better disguise its real, or latent, meaning. There is difficulty enough in Freud's description of secondary revision, however, even in *The Interpretation of Dreams*. This part of his theory depends heavily on his assumption that the manifest content of the dream is misleading and, by this device, becomes more so. We noticed, however, in dealing with the one documentable example of revision in the dream report (Dora's changing of "two and a half hours" to "two hours") that the result was exactly the opposite: the revised detail was more informative than its original. In effect, the revision substituted a symbolic detail for a literal one and, in so doing, better coordinated the multiple references of that detail to Dora's biography on the one hand and to the analytic situation on the other. After the least two chapters, we can make the same argument at a more general level: if the dream has been subjected to significant secondary revision, why does it so thoroughly fit the details of the case? What has been disguised? Given the cogency of the dream's representation of the analytic situation, it seems impossible to argue that significant secondary revision has disguised its real content. If there has been a significant degree of secondary revision, the result cannot be accounted for in Freud's theory and would require an entirely new description of that process of dream-work.

Finally, the possibility that Freud's handling of the dream texts altered them is a real one, but it is not a very serious threat to the claims of the aesthetic hypotheses, simply because the present form of the texts so well supports a non-Freudian reading. If Freud unconsciously modified the dream texts he did so against his own interests. Such a process would require a type of unconscious motivation on Freud's part—a self-defeating rather than a self-serving intention—that is not much in evidence elsewhere. Far more likely is the possibility that Freud's handling of the dream texts has rendered them less appropriate for the type of analysis we have been engaged in. We can safely assume that the texts have been simplified through the usual process of summary, for example, and that a fuller version would offer a great deal more detail than these versions do. Again, if there were at any point gaps or uncertainties in Freud's memory of the dreams as they were reported, we can assume that he either left those imperfections intact or corrected them according to his best understanding. In the first case he could hardly have improved the coherence of the dreams; in the second case, he would naturally have been guided by his own developing interpretation of the dream and the patient, and this would be most unlikely to produce material more favorable to our aesthetic reading than to his own reading.

In sum, it is quite possible that the texts of Dora's dreams have been modified to some degree by one or more of the factors we are discussing, but those factors would tend to produce modifications unfriendly to an aesthetic reading. By all the circumstantial evidence that we can muster—and it is the only type of evidence available for these questions—the most likely changes would have been ones that interfered with an attempt to discover aesthetic coherence in the dreams. This type of consideration is, precisely, part of the advantage of testing out our non-Freudian hypotheses on a Freudian example. We can be reassured on this score by both results of our analysis: that, on the one hand, we were able to discover the aesthetic dimension of a dream heard, remembered, and recorded by someone who categorically denied that dreams have any such quality; and that, on the other hand, the aesthetic interpretation fits so many of the facts of the case and even proposes a comprehensive and creditable explanation of those facts.

A broader treatment of many different dreams would help guard against the limitations of any single example, of course, and the next step in the investigation of the hypotheses of aesthetic coherence should be just such a study. There is no question but that further investigation is required. The approaches are complementary and both are necessary for a complete study of the hypotheses we have proposed. But surveys also entail limits of their own; it is impossible in a broader study to attend to any single dream as thoroughly as we have considered this one, to examine the number of details which we have been able to examine in this study. For a theory which claims both that the details of the manifest dream are significant and that a given interpretation of them can be confirmed by its ability to explain the specific harmony of those details, such an extended example as this one was essential. It is also true that Freud's very different interpretation is remarkably detailed in its own way, and any attempt to unravel it convincingly must be willing to work through those many specifics. We cannot help remember, too, the point made earlier about the intended position of this case history in the canon of Freud's exposition; he felt that *The Interpretation of Dreams* was incomplete precisely because it lacked just such a thorough demonstration of his theories, and the case history was written to fill this gap. This leaves us with the curious observation that, when called upon for an exhaustive model of his theory of interpretation, Freud could do no better than his work on Dora's dreams, and this, in turn, should make us eager to return to the numerous partial examples of *The Interpretation of Dreams* with a more critical eye. If the work in the preceding pages is convincing, we must conclude that nowhere in the twenty-three volumes of his works does Freud thoroughly exemplify the interpretive theories of his great work.

Horizons

The reflections of the last several paragraphs may lead us to wonder about the broader implications of our two hypotheses of aesthetic coherence; perhaps it would not be inappropriate to sketch out some related areas of interest even in a very cursory manner. Our study of Dora's dreams suggests four large topic areas which need to be explored in the light of a theory of the aesthetic coherence of dreams. The first and most obvious of these is the subject itself, the aesthetic dimension of dreams. Critical descriptions of specific aesthetic devices (to what extent do they *really* resemble the elements of literature?) and of the structures that can be found organizing them need to be carried out. Are some dreams more artistic than others? What are the crucial differences that distinguish the private aesthetic experience of the dream from the communicating and enlightening experience of a work of art? Is the dreamer, during his dream, more like an artist, an artist's audience, or both? Are there definable genres of dreams, distinguishable by aesthetic standards? Are there "pulp" dreams and "serious" dreams? Consideration of these and related topics will force the issue of the difference between the spoken or written record of a dream and its experienced reality and will also offer an approach to the question of the ego's distance from or involvement in that experience. Perhaps a study of the aesthetic dimension of dreams will help to explain why they are so often unintelligible, even to the dreamer, and why so often forgotten—if those are really two distinct topics.

A second subject, closely related to this first one, is a consideration of the implications of the analogy between dreams and art for our conception of art. Our understanding of and appreciation for art have been deeply influenced by Freud's theory of dreams and by his theory of art, which is nothing but an extension of the former. Subject matter, style, aesthetic theory, and taste have been affected by Freud's thinking; programmes have been built on his concepts; current popular assumptions about the nature and function of art have been biased by that influence.[6] Freudian theory has encouraged us to think of the work of art as a symptom or as a merely pleasureful diversion or as a screen hiding something more important than itself. It is true that Freud and his most astute successors have been very explicit about the boundaries of psychoanalytic thinking on this subject, and that they have made it very clear that psychoanalytic theory is not equipped to address the most interesting questions about the processes of artistic creation, the nature of the art work itself, or the complexities of an audience's response and appreciation. The pointedness of those reservations is all too clearly reflected in the work of those who have chosen to disregard them. The whole area stands, by almost universal acknowledgment, as one of the least satisfactorily developed dimensions of psychoanalytic thinking. But qualifications and self-imposed restraints notwithstanding, psychoanalysis has had its influence here. One reaction to that influence, and a method of addressing the questions it has raised, would be to reapply the Freudian equation (Art resembles Dream because both resemble Symptom) on an entirely new basis; if dreams are aesthetic productions, perhaps we can say that Art resembles Dream on the basis of their aesthetic dimension.[7] Instead of proposing that we are all neurotics in our sleep and children in our art, we might be able to say that we are artists in our sleep and dreamers in our art. At any rate, recognition of the aesthetic dimension of dreams will require us to refurbish some of our current attitudes about the status and function of art.

A third area for future research might be that of psychoanalytic theory itself since a major revision of Freud's theory of dreams is bound to have some impact on related topics. If dreams are a cornerstone of psychoanalytic theory, as Freud and others have considered them, and if dreams are not what Freud thought they were, then . . . ? With regard to his theory of dreams in particular, how would one negotiate between Freud's description of dream-work (with its purpose of disguising latent content) and the idea of an aesthetically coherent manifest dream? How would his theory of symbolism be affected? More fundamentally, what would be the status of the concept of latent content itself vis-à-vis such an understanding of the manifest dream? If the dream is indeed a "royal road to the unconscious," then where will this very different road lead us? It has often been said that *The Interpretation of Dreams*, and its seventh chapter in particular, contains the germ of nearly all of Freud's key concepts. It might well be true, then, that a substantial revision of Freud's dream theory would, like the first domino, touch off a chain reaction.

A fourth broad subject area suggests itself, since a shift in our conception of the dream implies a shift in the theory and methods of interpreting dreams. A question of hermeneutics is involved in both a specific and a general sense. Most immediately, a new method of dream interpretation would take its place among the individual subject matters and applications which are encompassed by a broad understanding of hermeneutics. In addition, however, current theories of interpretation have been influenced by Freud's thinking at least as much as current modes of art and a substantial recasting of Freud's dream theory ought to have some bearing on the current interest in hermeneutic questions.

These are large topics, clearly, and we mention them here not so much to reckon with them directly as to suggest that the horizons of this study of a single dream are not quite as narrow as they may have sometimes seemed. If dreams are aesthetic constructions and if, as some recent studies have suggested, they are not only more frequent but more necessary to our well-being than we once imagined, then dreams have something to tell us about ourselves which we have yet to fully understand. The "royal road" is open; we have barely begun to travel it.

Notes

Chapter One. Introduction

1. See Marie Jahoda, *Freud and the Dilemmas of Psychology* (New York: Basic Books, Inc., 1977), p. 37: "The ambition to create a general psychology stayed with Freud throughout his life. . . . Unless this is clearly understood it indeed 'remains a mystery why Freud should have treated the process of dreaming so seriously.' He did, because dreams were a bridge to general psychology." Jahoda is quoting a remark by Paul Roazen in *Sigmund Freud* (Englewood Cliffs, N.J.: Prentice-Hall, 1973), p. 4.

2. *The Interpretation of Dreams*, in *The Standard Edition of the Complete Psychological Works of Sigmund Freud*, ed. James Strachey, 24 vols. (London: The Hogarth Press, 1953–1974), 4:xxxii. All further references to Freud's work will be to this edition, abbreviated by *SE*, unless otherwise noted.

3. Ernest Jones, *The Life and Work of Sigmund Freud*, 3 vols. (New York: Basic Books, Inc., 1953–1957), 1:350–351 (hereafter cited as *Life*).

4. "The theory of dreams . . . is without doubt the best founded portion of the whole psychoanalytic theory" (Franz Alexander, "About Dreams with Unpleasant Content," *Psychiatric Quarterly* 4 [1930]: 447). See also Jahoda, *Freud and the Dilemmas of Psychology*, p. 38: *The Interpretation of Dreams*, she says, "contains, sometimes in embryonic form, sometimes fully elaborated, virtually all

the major psychological concepts of psychoanalysis, even though some of them were to undergo drastic revision later on."

5. Thus David R. Hawkins claims, "Except for slight additions in *A Metapsychological Supplement to the Theory of Dreams* (Freud, 1917) there was little further development by Freud of his concepts of the dream process. . . . The chief further developments were in pointing out the role the superego plays in dream formation" ("A Review of Psychoanalytic Dream Theory in the Light of Recent Psycho-physiological Studies of Sleep and Dreaming," *British Journal of Medical Psychology* 39 [1966]: 85).

6. Ibid.

7. Hanns Sachs, *Freud: Master and Friend* (Freeport, N.Y.: Books for Libraries Press, 1970), pp. 60–61.

8. Gregory Zilboorg, *Sigmund Freud: His Exploration of the Mind of Man* (New York: Charles Scribner's Sons, 1951), p. 1.

9. Leon L. Altman, *The Dream in Psychoanalysis* (New York: International Universities Press, 1975), pp. 1–2. On the varying status of dream interpretation in psychoanalytic thinking and practice, see, in addition to Altman, Erik H. Erikson, "The Dream Specimen of Psychoanalysis," in *Psychoanalytic Psychiatry and Psychology*, ed. R. Knight and C. Friedman (New York: International Universities Press, 1954), pp. 131–170; L. Rangell, reporter, "Panel Report: The Dream in the Practice of Psychoanalysis," *Journal of the American Psychoanalytic Association* 4 (1956):122–137; H. F. Waldhorn, "The Place of the Dream in Clinical Psychoanalysis," *Kris Study Group Monograph* 2 (1967):96–105; R. R. Greenson, "The Exceptional Position of the Dream in Psycho-Analytic Practice," *Psychoanalytic Quarterly* 39 (1970):519–549; Alan Roland, "The Context and Unique Function of Dreams in Psychoanalytic Therapy: Clinical Approach," *International Journal of Psychoanalysis* 52 (1971):431–439; H. P. Blum, "The Changing Use of Dreams in Psychoanalytic Practice: Dreams and Free Association," *International Journal of Psychoanalysis* 57 (1976):315–324; M. Masud R. Khan, "The Changing Use of Dreams in Psychoanalytic Practice: In Search of the Dreaming Experience," *International Journal of Psychoanalysis* 57 (1976):325–330;

E. Hartmann, "Discussion of 'The Changing Use of Dreams in Psychoanalytic Practice': The Dream as the 'Royal Road' to the Biology of the Mental Apparatus," *International Journal of Psychoanalysis* 57 (1976):331–334; Carlos Plata-Mújica, "Discussion of 'The Changing Use of Dreams in Psychoanalytic Practice,'" *International Journal of Psychoanalysis* 57 (1976):335–341; H. C. Curtis and D. M. Sachs, reporters, "Dialogue on 'The Changing Use of Dreams in Psychoanalytic Practice,'" *International Journal of Psychoanalysis* 57 (1976):343–354; and Joseph M. Natterson, ed., *The Dream in Clinical Practice* (New York: Jason Aronson, 1980). Given the prominence of the dream and its interpretation in Freud's theory, the very existence of "an increasing controversy over the place of the dream in psychoanalysis" is in itself both curious and intriguing (Roland, "Dreams in Psychoanalytic Therapy," p. 431). Occasional references to the number of dreams an analyst is forced to leave uninterpreted also suggest the degree to which classical Freudian interpretation depends on intuitive insight even more than on any objectifiable methodology—a point made very clear by Thomas M. French and Erika Fromm, *Dream Interpretation: A New Approach* (New York: Basic Books, Inc., 1964).

10. David Foulkes, *A Grammar of Dreams* (New York: Basic Books, Inc., 1978), p. 27.

11. Small indications are symptomatic. Several writers have commented on the desirability of aligning Freud's theory of dreams more precisely with his dynamic structure (id, ego, superego) since those concepts received their fullest development after the presentation of his dream theory in terms of his earlier, topographical division (unconscious, preconscious, conscious). No one has done so, however. Or again, it is curious that two seminal works in the development of ego psychology scarcely mention dreams; I am thinking of Anna Freud's *The Ego and the Mechanisms of Defense* (New York: International Universities Press, 1966) and Heinz Hartmann's *Ego Psychology and the Problem of Adaptation* (New York: International Universities Press, 1939). If the defense mechanisms which Anna Freud describes serve multiple and simultaneous

functions of adaptation, inhibition, and synthesis (Heinz Hartmann, *Ego Psychology*, p. 51), is it not possible that the devices of the dreamwork operate with similarly multiple purposes?

12. "Our first step in the employment of this procedure teaches us that what we must take as the object of our attention is not the dream as a whole but the separate portions of its content. . . . I put the dream before him [the patient] and cut it up into pieces. . . . Thus the method of dream interpretation which I practise . . . employs interpretation *en détail* and not *en masse* . . . it regards dreams from the very first as being of a composite character, as being conglomerates of psychical formations" (Freud, *The Interpretation of Dreams*, SE 4:103–104). Freud maintained this principle with perfect consistency; see, for example, the *Introductory Lectures*: "In general one must avoid seeking to explain one part of the manifest dream by another, as though the dream had been coherently conceived and was a logically arranged narrative. On the contrary, it is as a rule like a piece of breccia, composed of various fragments of rock held together by a binding medium, so that the designs that appear on it do not belong to the original rocks embedded in it" (*SE* 15:181–182). The key word in the first of these sentences is, of course, "logically"; a narrative may be "arranged" or ordered on the basis of principles other than logical ones. More obviously, non-narrative art forms may organize their components coherently without resorting to logic. The famous metaphor in the second sentence of this quotation is, one realizes, no argument at all against the coherence of the surface "designs" of the dream, however they may relate to the "original rocks."

13. "Dreams occur which, at a superficial view, may seem faultlessly logical and reasonable; they start from a possible situation, carry it on through a chain of consistent modifications and—though far less frequently—bring it to a conclusion which causes no surprise. Dreams which are of such a kind have been subjected to a far-reaching revision by this psychical function that is akin to waking thought [i.e., secondary revision]; they appear to have a mean-

ing, but that meaning is as far removed as possible from their true significance" (Freud, *The Interpretation of Dreams*, SE 5:490).

14. For convenient and comprehensive reviews of this work see, in addition to Foulkes, *Grammar of Dreams*; Milton Kramer, ed., *Dream Psychology and the New Biology of Dreaming* (Springfield, Ill.: Charles C. Thomas, 1969); William C. Dement, *Some Must Watch While Some Must Sleep* (New York: W. W. Norton & Co., 1976); and Richard M. Jones, *The New Psychology of Dreaming* (New York: Penguin Books, 1978).

15. Freud, *Introductory Lectures*, SE 15:83. The equation was crucial to Freud's thinking and he frequently made use of it. Thus, later in the *Introductory Lectures*, "A healthy person, too, is virtually a neurotic; but dreams appear to be the only symptoms which he is capable of forming" (Ibid. 16:457). Freud acknowledges that his explanation of dreaming had its source in his study of the neuroses (Ibid. 15:83) and claims, of course, that dreams cannot be understood except in terms of their similarity to neurotic symptoms: "But just as dreams prepare the way to an understanding of the neuroses, so, on the other hand, a true appreciation of dreams can only be achieved after a knowledge of neurotic phenomena" (Ibid., p. 239). This whole topic is worth more attention than we can give to it here; the analysis of Dora's second dream which follows certainly suggests a need to reexamine the equation between dream and symptom.

16. Altman, *Dream in Psychoanalysis*, p. 10.

17. Foulkes, *Grammar of Dreams*, p. 96.

18. Most notable, of course, is the work of Calvin Hall whose methodology, although entirely different from Freud's, is almost equally effective in precluding consideration of manifest coherence. In general, content analysts prefer to deal with a summary description of a dream's features, or with a list of features; they seldom examine the internal relationship of one dream element to another nor do they have access to any analytical tool suitable for exploring aesthetic features. See, for example, Calvin S. Hall, *The Meaning of Dreams* (New York: McGraw Hill Book Co., 1966) and Calvin S.

Hall and Vernon J. Nordby, *The Individual and His Dreams* (New York: New American Library, 1972).

19. In general terms, any consideration of the dream which implies that it is an identifiable entity which can be characterized as a whole goes some way towards my hypotheses. Thus, for example, a viewpoint which emphasizes a communicative function or a problem-solving function for the dream as a whole implies some degree of coherence in the dream; again, the assignment of a single theme to a dream or the claim that dreams in a series are thematically related are arguments that depend on the assumption that a dream is, to some degree, a unified entity.

20. The concurrent fact is that those equipped for a properly aesthetic analysis have not had sufficient command of psychoanalytic theory, so that even so valuable a study as Meredith Anne Skura's recent *The Literary Use of the Psychoanalytic Process* (New Haven: Yale University Press, 1981) must rely on Freud's theory as it stands —without addressing its internal difficulties—in order to draw an enlightening analogy between dreams and allegory. The situation which Edward Glover described in 1950 remains substantially the same, in spite of more imaginative approaches in recent years: "Particularly in the field of aesthetics, Freudian formulations have been strictly limited to pointing out the infantile and unconscious origins of the sublimatory process and the part played by creative sublimations in preventing, controlling or assuaging unconscious conflict, in other words, in helping to maintain peace of mind. Beyond that the Freudian has not seen fit to go. Nor, to put it quite frankly, is the average analyst qualified to do so. Like most psychiatrists, he has neither the cultural feeling nor the type of education necessary to pursue these matters beyond the limits of his professional vision" (*Freud or Jung* [London: George Allen & Unwin, Ltd., 1950], p. 12).

21. A catalogue of references and analogies can be found in F. C. Prescott's essay, "Poetry and Dreams," *Journal of Abnormal and Social Psychology* 7 (1912):17–46, 104–143; on this article see Claudia A. Morrison, *Freud and the Critic: The Early Use of Depth Psychology*

in Literary Criticism (Chapel Hill: University of North Carolina Press, 1968), pp. 51–57. Ella Freeman Sharpe uses analogies between dream devices and rhetorical devices in a fairly extensive but purely illustrative way in *Dream Analysis* (London: The Hogarth Press, 1961), chapter 2.

22. Calvin S. Hall, "Diagnosing Personality by the Analysis of Dreams," *Journal of Abnormal and Social Psychology* 42 (1947):68–79.

Chapter Two. The Art of Dora's Dream

1. Freud, "Fragment of an Analysis of a Case of Hysteria," *SE* 7:3–122 (hereafter cited in the text as *Dora*).

2. Freud, *The Origins of Psycho-Analysis. Letters to Wilhelm Fliess, Drafts and Notes: 1887–1902*, ed. Marie Bonaparte, Anna Freud, Ernst Kris, trans. Eric Mosbacher and James Strachey (New York: Basic Books, Inc., 1954), p. 326.

3. Ernest Jones, *Life* 1:363.

4. How closely the two works were linked in Freud's mind may be indicated by a curious parapraxis: "Contemporary evidence is therefore conclusive about the date of the analysis. Yet in 1914 and again in 1923 Freud three times gives a wrong date, placing it a year earlier than it actually was. It is permissible to suggest that his lapse of memory came from the connection in his mind between the essay and *The Interpretation of Dreams* (which the publisher also misdated by a year), since it had closely corresponded with the chapter of the same title he had intended to insert in that book" (Ernest Jones, *Life* 1:363). Arnold A. Rogow offers an alternate explanation: "But another hypothesis is that Freud, following the exchange with Fliess at Achensee in the summer of 1900 about the origins of the concept of bisexuality, unconsciously wished to keep as far apart as possible the dates of Dora's analysis—in which bisexuality played a key role—and the discussion with Fliess" ("A Further Footnote to Freud's 'Fragment of an Analysis of a Case of Hysteria,'" *Journal of the American Psychoanalytic Association* 26 [1978]:335).

5. Frank J. Sulloway, *Freud: Biologist of the Mind* (New York: Basic Books, Inc., 1979), pp. 345–346.

6. Steven Marcus, "Freud and Dora: Story, History, Case History, " in *Representations* (New York: Random House, 1975), p. 260.

7. Foulkes makes much the same point: "*The Interpretation of Dreams* does not, in fact, illustrate Freud's full and final approach to dream explanation, in which associations are traced back to childhood sexual situations and in which the dream is placed in a narrative consisting of the dreamer's entire life-history. For this sort of analysis, one needs to turn to Freud's few written accounts of his patients' case histories" (*Grammar of Dreams*, p. 37). The point had also been made by Thomas M. French (*The Integration of Behavior. II: The Integrative Process in Dreams* [Chicago: University of Chicago Press, 1954], p. 12, n. 6).

8. Ernest Jones, *Life* 1:364; Sulloway, *Freud: Biologist of the Mind*, p. 346; Philip Rieff, ed., "Introduction," in Sigmund Freud, *Dora: An Analysis of a Case of Hysteria* (New York: Collier Books, 1963), p. 9; Marcus, "Freud and Dora," p. 268.

9. "In every analysis there are dreams which, like rubrics, indicate the course the analysis is likely to follow. These dreams express the main conflicts as well as the relative capacity of the ego to cope with them" (Milton L. Miller, "Ego Functioning in Two Types of Dreams," *Psychoanalytic Quarterly*, 17 [1948]:346). On the communicative function of the dream in relation to the transference see, for example, Sandor Ferenczi, "To Whom Does One Relate One's Dreams?" in *Further Contributions to the Theory and Technique of Psychoanalysis* (London: The Hogarth Press, 1950); Mark Kanzer, "The Communicative Function of the Dream," *International Journal of Psychoanalysis* 36 (1955):260–266; M. S. Bergmann, "The Intrapsychic and Communicative Aspects of the Dream," *International Journal of Psychoanalysis* 47 (1966):356–363; John Klauber, "On the Significance of Reporting Dreams in Psycho-analysis," *International Journal of Psychoanalysis* 48 (1967):424–432; and Harold Stewart, "The Experiencing of the Dream and the Transference," *International Journal of Psychoanalysis* 54 (1973):345–347.

10. Marcus's well-known essay ("Freud and Dora") undertakes a literary analysis of the case history itself, rather than the dreams, which occupy a small part of his attention; his thorough treatment of several major structural and stylistic devices illuminates both the case history and its author. Stanley Edgar Hyman catalogues a few of the important metaphors in Freud's text (*The Tangled Bark* [New York: Atheneum, 1962], pp. 344–345).

Our exposition of the aesthetic features of Dora's dream is not entirely unprecedented, although the subject has never been addressed in detail. John L. Schimel, however, cites a dream which he is able to term "aesthetically pleasing. It works even as a piece of literature. With small revisions it could emerge as poetry. Its themes are not only personal but transpersonal" ("The Semantic and Aesthetic Analyses of Dreams," in *Dream Dynamics*, ed. Jules H. Masserman [New York: Grune & Stratton, 1971], p. 12).

11. This procedure, which radically violates Freud's insistence upon the need for associations in order to interpret a dream, is not, it seems, quite so radical in comparison to actual practice. See, for example, Jacob Spanjaard, "The Manifest Dream Content and Its Significance for the Interpretation of Dreams," *International Journal of Psychoanalysis* 50 (1969): "It is striking how many analysts will interpret a dream directly from the manifest content and without associations, especially when they know the patient well" (p. 227). Spanjaard cites Rangell ("Panel Report: The Dream in Psychoanalysis") and Charlotte G. Babcock ("Panel Report: The Manifest Content of the Dream," *Journal of the American Psychoanalytic Association* 14 [1966]:154–171). We can also be encouraged by Richard M. Jones's comments: "There is much room in the study of dreams for approaches other than the epigenetic, especially those that emphasize adaptation to *external* realities: time, space, physical causality, culture patterns, etc. In this the structure of manifest dreams should remain the research material of choice . . . the parameters of such research will be best derived from theories other than psychoanalytic" (*Ego Synthesis in Dreams* [Cambridge, Mass.: Schenkman Publishing Co., 1962], p. 82).

12. In quoting the dream text I have modified it by dividing it into paragraphs and by incorporating into the text itself the five addenda which Dora supplied in the sessions in which she and Freud discussed the dream. The addenda are printed in brackets. There seems to me no question about the placement of any of the five unless there is a possibility of reversing the last two sentences, which were apparently added separately by Dora. Unfortunately, Freud gives little indication of the exact timing or analytical contexts of the addenda.

13. Freud acknowledges the importance of such structural aspects of the manifest dream, but only insofar as they correspond to latent elements: "The number of part-dreams into which a dream is divided usually corresponds to the number of main topics or groups of thoughts in the latent dream. . . . Thus the form of dreams is far from being without significance and itself calls for interpretation" (*The Introductory Lectures to Psychoanalysis*, SE 15:177). Freud does not address this aspect of Dora's dream, as we shall see in the next chapter. Even if he had, our objective here would still be quite different, of course: we want to see how structural considerations illuminate the relationships *among manifest elements*, before considering corresponding latent elements. The same distinction should be made in regard to Erikson's important study of manifest content ("Dream Specimen in Psychoanalysis") and to Iago Galdston's article, "Dream Morphology: Its Diagnostic and Prognostic Significance," *American Journal of Psychiatry* 109 (1952):287–290.

14. Shlomo Breznitz ("A Critical Note on Secondary Revision," *International Journal of Psychoanalysis* 52 [1971]:411) mentions "those dreams in which a certain part appears intelligible and integrated into a story, after which comes a meaningless, disordered section, and then again better ordering. It looks as if PR [primary revision—that phase of Freud's secondary revision which operates while the dream is being constructed (p. 409)] was contributing on different levels to the dream content throughout the dream." He does not, however, consider the possibility of functional stylistic or structural variation.

15. See Daniel E. Schneider, "Time-Space and the Growth of the Sense of Reality: A Contribution to the Psychophysiology of the Dream," *Psychoanalytic Review* 35 (1948):229–252, for an application of "time-space" concepts to dreams.

16. Freud, *The Interpretation of Dreams*, SE 5:385.

17. On this point, as on several others, we are limited by a lack of detail in the dream text. It would be very helpful to know, for example, more about each of Dora's rooms and the extent to which they were similar or different from each other. Each of them is termed "my room," and it may be that the dream presented Dora with recognizable versions of her own room (present or past), or that one or both rooms were significantly different from any real room of hers, or that one or both were too vaguely realized in the dream to allow a determination. Had the dream report been received by someone interested in the integrity of the manifest dream, or even its relative completeness, more detail might have been recovered: "The dreamer, when asked, often can remember more details than he has given in his original account. It may be fruitful, also, to ask for specific aspects of the dream which seem to be missing or incomplete, such as the setting of the dream or the identity of a figure" (Mary Ann Mattoon, *Applied Dream Analysis: A Jungian Approach* [Washington, D.C.: V. H. Winston & Sons, 1978], p. 52). The whole question of textual reliability is a complicated one, however, and requires separate treatment. Stuart C. Miller offers a pointed illustration of the summary nature of most dream reports, using one of Freud's dreams ("The Manifest Dream and the Appearance of Color in Dreams," *International Journal of Psychoanalysis* 45 [1964]:514–517).

18. The dream's heavy reliance on paradox (which is further examined in the details of the next two chapters) offers us a good concrete example of a phenomenon that has bedeviled psychoanalytic attempts at aesthetic questions. Pinchas Noy comments: "This last ability of art—that of simultaneously expressing different and at times contradictory meanings—bears on a phenomenon known in the theory of communication as double-bind communication, and

regarded as a pathological phenomenon" ("About Art and Artistic Talent," *International Journal of Psychoanalysis* 53 [1972]:244). Noy goes on to emphasize the frequent and important use of paradox and ambiguity in art on the conscious level. Without the corrective of such a viewpoint, however, it would be all too easy to liken dream paradoxes to the pathological phenomena of double-bind communication (thus confirming the "pathological" nature of dreams) without considering their aesthetic and integrative potential. But see, for example, Plata-Mújica, "Discussion of 'The Changing Use of Dreams,'" p. 340: "Dreams are liable to be used paradoxically, due to the fact that in them everything may or may not be at the same time." Robert Rogers examines a poem of George Herbert's in a precise and reliable analysis of aesthetic paradox and ambiguity ("On the Metapsychology of Poetic Language: Modal Ambiguity," *International Journal of Psychoanalysis* 54 [1973]:61–74), and Roland suggests the psychological scope of these devices in dreams: "Thus dreams have the makings of effective paradoxes, where contradictory lines of thought are synthesized into a fuller truth related to the relevant context" ("Dreams in Psychoanalytic Therapy," p. 433). But in a later article Roland fails to exploit the parallel use of paradox in dreams and art ("Imagery and Symbolic Expression in Dreams and Art," *International Journal of Psychoanalysis* 53 [1972]:536).

19. Perhaps the most ambitious attempts to explore the coherence of the manifest dream thus far have been in the work of Marshall Edelson ("Language and Dreams: *The Interpretation of Dreams* Revisited," *The Psychoanalytic Study of the Child* 27 [1972]:203–282; *Language and Interpretation in Psychoanalysis* [New Haven: Yale University Press, 1975]) and Foulkes (*Grammar of Dreams*), who have proposed that dream coherence is founded in or analogous to linguistic principles. Foulkes, for example, states, "*We* must note that the manifest dream experience *is* created under the evident influences of *the intention of coherence of the dramatic narrative*; thus any comprehensive explanation of that experience must invoke

waking-type principles of syntactic organization" (p. 72, his emphasis) and, in reference to any analogy used by Freud, "That analogy—dreaming is like writing a poem—seems to me exact" (p. 72). The "syntax" of dreams, though, is a linguistic rather than an aesthetic topic, and so quite different from the interests of my investigation. More recently Foulkes has proposed a model of dream creation based on psycholinguistics; see his "A Cognitive-Psychological Model of REM Dream Production," *Sleep* 5 (1982):169–187.

Chapter Three. Freud on Dora's Dream

1. "Dora" was actually Ida Bauer. Her fictional name was suggested to Freud by the circumstances of a nursemaid who worked for Freud's sister; since both were named "Rosa," the servant was asked to use another name and chose "Dora," as Freud recounts in *The Psychopathology of Everyday Life* (*SE* 6:240–241). Hannah S. Decker argues that Freud was also influenced by certain analogies between Ida Bauer and "Anna O.," the subject of the case history by Breuer in *Studies in Hysteria*, Josef Breuer and Sigmund Freud, ed. and trans. by James Strachey (*SE* 2). Decker points out that Breuer had a daughter named Dora; see her "The Choice of a Name: 'Dora' and Freud's Relationship with Breuer," *Journal of the American Psychoanalytic Association*, 30 (1982):113–136. Marcus offers the alternate (or additional) explanation that Freud was thinking of Dora in Charles Dickens's *David Copperfield* ("Freud and Dora," p. 309, n. 26).

Felix Deutsch recounts his interview with and evaluation of Dora some twenty-one years after her analysis with Freud in "A Footnote to Freud's 'Fragment of an Analysis of a Case of Hysteria,'" *Psychoanalytic Quarterly* 26 (1957):159–167; Rogow supplies biographical information about Dora's brother in "A Further Footnote."

2. Freud's interpretation of this symptom stands as one of his classic examples of displacement (*Dora*, pp. 28–32), but see Franz

Alexander, *Fundamentals of Psychoanalysis* (New York: W. W. Norton & Co., 1963), p. 247. Richard Wollheim elaborates somewhat on the cough in *Sigmund Freud* (Cambridge: Cambridge University Press, 1971), pp. 97–98.

 3. See Henri F. Ellenberger: "These studies by Krafft-Ebing and others provoked a deep interest that soon reached a wide public, which, as we have seen, was already provided with a great number of novels on the subject of sex. Contrary to the present-day legend that would have us believe that those were days of sexual obscurantism, on the Continent there were no barriers to the publication, distribution of, and access to such writings. It was also the time when popular books on sexual matters began to appear everywhere. . . . [Moritz] Benedikt adds that Mantegazza, an Italian professor, published a book on sexual matters that also became a best seller and was translated into several languages, and justified himself by saying that, because of his modest remuneration as a professor, he had to find other sources of income" (*The Discovery of the Unconscious* [New York: Basic Books, Inc., 1970], pp. 298–299). The third edition of a German translation by Dr. Eduard Engel of Mantegazza's *Physiology of Love* was published in 1889, for example (Jena: Hermann Costenoble).

 4. Freud, *The Origins of Psycho-Analysis*, p. 325.

 5. French (*Integration of Behavior*, p. 14) accepts Freud's interpretation of the jewel case but adds, "The jewel case is one that Dora received as a gift from Mr. K. It is an acceptable symbol that refers most obviously to her tender attachment to him." Freud reads the symbol sexually, noting that "*Schmuckkästchen*" "is a favourite expression for . . . the female genitals" as well as meaning "jewel-case" (*Dora*, p. 69).

 6. Marcus, "Freud and Dora," p. 292.

 7. Later in the analysis Freud will express his surprise and disappointment at Dora's termination even though, according to the note we have just quoted, he predicted that event himself, "a few" weeks beforehand, as Marcus observes ("Freud and Dora,", p. 304).

 8. When Dora first had the dream she was still able to look to her

father for help. By the time the dream reappeared during analysis, however, Dora no longer regarded her father as a potential savior (as will become obvious in our analysis of her second dream). In fact, at this time Dora numbered her father among her betrayers because he had taken Herr K.'s side against hers, in the matter of the proposition, for transparently selfish motives. Insofar as the dream refers to Dora's contemporary situation (rather than revivifying a past one, which it clearly also does), then, it seems to refer to a contemporary father-figure who might save her from a contemporary "fire," as she had hoped her father would have saved her from Herr K.'s "fire" two years ago. If the dream means to cast Freud in this role, then his position changes drastically between this dream and the second one.

9. Freud's conflation of separate scenes is also evident in his reference to the forest scene in the dream as "the first situation in the dream" when, in fact, it is the second (*Dora*, p. 99). Freud seems to consider the first two scenes of the dream as one part and the third scene as a second part, though he does not observe that division consistently either.

10. It is disappointing, of course, that Freud does not attend to the "monument in one of the squares," although that masculine symbol would be difficult to reconcile with his casting of Dora in a masculine role. Jacques Lacan emphasizes Dora's masculine identification, too, apparently on the basis of this proposal of Freud's; see Lacan's "Intervention on Transference," in *Feminine Sexuality*, ed. Juliet Mitchell and Jacqueline Rose (New York: W. W. Norton & Co., 1982), pp. 61–73.

11. On Freud's own railway phobia and on the railway metaphors he used in this case history and elsewhere, see Bertram D. Lewin, "The Train Ride: A Study of One of Freud's Figures of Speech," *Psychoanalytic Quarterly* 39 (1970):71–89.

12. See Neil Hertz, "Dora's Secrets, Freud's Techniques," *Diacritics* 13, no. 1 (1983):73.

13. "Dream images generally are sequenced in such a manner as to lend thematic coherence to their progression. The dream is a

drama, and, as such, has a tightly woven inner structure" (Foulkes, *Grammar of Dreams*, p. 14).

14. "The sensation of the inhibition of a movement represents a *conflict of will*. . . . Now an impulse transmitted along the motor paths is nothing other than a volition, and the fact of our being so certain that we shall feel that impulse inhibited during sleep is what makes the whole process so admirably suited for representing an act of volition and a 'no' which opposes it" (Freud, *The Interpretation of Dreams*, SE 4:337).

15. The last two sentences of the translation are from Rieff's edition, *Dora: An Analysis of a Case of Hysteria*, p. 83. The Strachey translation of them in the *Standard Edition* reads: "Four more nights. On the following day I went away with Father" (*Dora*, p. 66).

16. Unfortunately, Freud does not date this visit or supply the information that would allow us to fix it in Dora's chronology.

17. Dora apparently related the dream during what turned out to be the antepenultimate session. That session was followed by a second, also spent on interpreting the dream, and by a third, the last, on December 31, 1900, which was also spent on the dream. It was at the beginning of this last session that Dora announced her previously formed intention of breaking off the analysis. Freud notes the "two hours" parallel in the postscript to the case history (*Dora*, p. 119).

18. The editor's note in the *Standard Edition* (pp. 5–6) untangles the chronology of the case history:

1882	Dora born.
*1888 (age 6)	Father ill with T.B. Family move to B——.
1889 (age 7)	Bedwetting.
*1890 (age 8)	Dyspnoea.
*1892 (age 10)	Father's detached retina.
*1894 (age 12)	Father's confusional attack. His visit to Freud [for treatment of syphilis]. Migraine and tussis nervosa.
*1896 (age 14)	Scene of the kiss.

*1898 (age 16)	(Early summer): Dora's first visit to Freud.	
	(End of June): Scene by the lake.	
	(Winter): Death of Aunt. Dora in Vienna.	
1899 (age 17)	(March): Appendicitis.	
	(Autumn): Family leave B—— and move to factory town.	
*1900 (age 18)	Family move to Vienna. Suicide threat.	
	(October to December): Treatment with Freud.	
1901 (age 19)	(January): Case history written.	
*1902 (age 20)	(April): Dora's last visit to Freud.	

The asterisks mark events in the two-year pattern.

19. "Whenever data like 'six p. m.,' 'eight-thirty,' or 'September twenty-sixth,' appear in dreams, they express the distortion of an object relationship highly charged with emotion. In analysis the reference is usually to the transference relationship. . . . The displacement from the person to time is the result of ambivalence or guilt regarding the id impulse which is connected with the object relationship" (Alfred Gross, "A Sense of Time in Dreams," *Psychoanalytic Quarterly* 18 (1949):467). Whether or not this claim can be accepted categorically, it accurately describes the significance of the specific time references in Dora's second dream.

20. Freud noted to Dora, "You waited for that length of time so as to see whether he would repeat his proposals; if he had, you would have concluded that he was in earnest, and did not mean to play with you as he had done with the governess" (*Dora*, p. 107). If this was true, it did not alter the fact that the two-week period was the time required to *resolve the conflict* which was, to some degree, a conflict between Dora's desire for Herr K. and her fear that his proposal to her was no more substantial than his proposal to the young governess had been. The experience of the governess suggested a frightening paradox: if Dora accepted Herr K. she might thereby lose him, as the governess had. If, however, Herr K. had come forward with a serious, public proposal during this two weeks'

"notice," that particular conflict (admittedly not the only one involved) would have been resolved.

21. "If the first account given me by a patient of a dream is too hard to follow I ask him to repeat it. In doing so he rarely uses the same words. But the parts of the dream which he describes in different terms are by that fact revealed to me as the weak spot in the dream's disguise. . . . under pressure of the resistance . . . he hastily covers the weak spots in the dream's disguise by replacing any expressions that threaten to betray its meaning by other less revealing ones. In this way he draws my attention to the expression which he has dropped out" (Freud, *The Interpretation of Dreams*, SE 5:515).

22. For example, Freud writes two pages later: "The numerous questions which she had been raising latterly seem to have been belated derivatives of questions inspired by the sexual curiosity which she had tried to gratify with the encyclopaedia" (*Dora*, p. 104, n. 2). Granted Dora's childhood sexual research is a reasonable hypothesis, but the issue is complicated by the fact that elsewhere Freud identifies two other sources of Dora's sexual knowledge—Frau K. and the governess her father had employed—both of them important to the subject matter of the dream.

23. Connections between the book and the letter (implied in the previous chapter) can also be made. The limp which Dora does not have in the dream links the book to the encyclopedia in which she read about the symptoms of appendicitis which she combined with her limp; she was sent to that encyclopedia by a letter about her cousin's appendicitis (*Dora*, p. 101). Again, the book is ironically juxtaposed in the dream against her mother's letter which invites her home or, in a way, back from the lakeside scene; this should be linked with the young governess's letter from her parents telling her that since she had not left her own lakeside scene, she could not return home. Dora's symptom joined a "false pregnancy" (appendicitis) with a limp; the dream pairs the book (appendicitis, no limp) with a letter (temptation refused). Dora's suicide letter should also be set in this context.

24. Kanzer's remark applies to this and several other key images in Dora's dream: "A single dream image may embody a complicated harmony of past and contemporary relationships and communications—viz., the 'R. is my uncle' dream of Freud, which condenses an exchange of opinions among several persons and is climaxed by a message to the dreamer himself" ("Communicative Function of Dreams," p. 261). Jules Glenn, after reviewing several of Freud's case histories, supports Kanzer's thinking: "Hence while insisting that dreams are primarily unconscious disguised wish fulfillments, a cherished belief, Freud also revealed the clinical significance of the dream as an expression of intent. As such he adumbrated Kanzer's (1955) study of the communicative function of the dream" ("Notes on Psychoanalytic Concepts and Style in Freud's Case Histories," in *Freud and His Patients*, ed. Mark Kanzer and Jules Glenn [New York: Jason Aronson, 1978], p. 17).

The "overdetermined" symbol of the book also raises the question of controlled ambiguity in dreams as opposed to art. In his famous essay on "Aesthetic Ambiguity," Ernst Kris distinguishes between the ambiguity of dreams and that of art on the basis of ego control of the regression in the two cases: "The regression in the case of aesthetic creation—in contrast to these other cases [i.e., fantasy, dream, and states of intoxication and fatigue]—is purposive and controlled" (*Psychoanalytic Explorations in Art* [London: Allen & Unwin, Ltd., 1953], p. 253). Kris would say that the ambiguity of the dream symbol has been accomplished without the purposeful control of the ego. Nonetheless, ambiguity in this dream (once we are in a position to gauge it) operates with all the appearance of intentionality, like an artistic device. It is certainly purposeful and coherent within the dream. Thus the distinction between dreams and art which Kris is so intent on maintaining seems to require some adjustment.

25. There will be no confusion on a point like this one, we assume, between the dream's presentation and Dora's actual or future condition. Our positive reading of this symbol (Freud would, no

doubt, interpret it by reversal) is justified by the manifest text, by the aesthetic congruity between this detail and the dream as a whole. The fact that the dream might propose a formulation distinct from, or even contrary to, the current psychological realities of the dreamer instantly raises a cluster of theoretical questions, none of which are satisfactorily answered by, for example, Jung's theory of the compensatory function of dreams (Jung, *Dreams*, trans. R.F.C. Hull [Princeton: Princeton University Press, 1974], pp. 37ff., 74ff., and 101ff.). Deutsch ("A Footnote") describes Dora's personality and circumstances twenty-one years after her analysis with Freud and summarizes her life history. She retained the symptomatic limp which the dream image "cures." It should also be noted that—although Freud makes no mention of it in the case history—he considered stair climbing in dreams as symbolic of sexual intercourse (*The Interpretation of Dreams*, SE 5:355, n. 2, 369–371) and reports one of his own dreams in which his movement was paralyzed (*SE* 4:238–240).

26. There is yet another connection to be made here, and it concerns the governess who treated Dora well only as a means of winning her father's attention and whom Dora caused to be fired once she realized the woman had no real interest in her: "This governess used to read every sort of book on sexual life and similar subjects, and talked to the girl about them, at the same time asking her quite frankly not to mention their conversations to her parents, as one could never tell what line they might take about them. For some time I looked upon this woman as the source of all Dora's secret knowledge, and perhaps I was not entirely wrong in this" (*Dora*, p. 36n).

27. "The great explanatory power of Freud's dream-work processes is *semantic*. These processes enable us to explain the referents of discrete dream images, to unravel the sources from which we believe their meaning derives. The great explanatory shortcoming of such processes is *syntactic*. They do not explain a central fact of dream experience: how such multi-determined images are put to-

gether in the form of coherent dramatic episodes, stories with sensible beginnings, middles, and ends" (Foulkes, *Grammar of Dreams*, p. 71).

28. Freud indicates here that the order of presentation in the case history should not be mistaken for the order of the analysis itself; Marcus supports the same conclusion when he examines the literary artifice of the case history. The fact that Freud has given the written document its own order makes Lacan's analysis difficult, since Lacan tries to impose a rhetorical organization which, however, he says "is not a mere contrivance for presenting material whose emergence Freud clearly states here is left to the will of the patient" ("Intervention on Transference," p. 64). Lacan's schema of dialectical reversals, therefore, is a more reliable guide to Freud's mind than to Dora's, nor can we even be confident that it charts the progress of the actual analysis from Freud's point of view. As we will see in the next chapter, the "conception of the case history" which Lacan calls "*identical* to the progress of the subject, that is, to the reality of the treatment" (p. 64) varies markedly according to the point of view—Freud's or Dora's—adopted.

29. Marcus offers the most thorough discussion of the various ways in which the case history is "fragmentary" ("Freud and Dora," pp. 265–270).

30. Freud makes the point in relation to symptoms: "It is not necessary for the various meanings of a symptom to be compatible with one another, that is, to fit together into a connected whole. It is enough that the unity should be constituted by the subject-matter which has given rise to all the various phantasies" (*Dora*, p. 53).

31. Freud does not always interpret death in a dream as literally as he does in this instance, as can be seen in the example of a girl who dreamed she saw her nephew dead, which Freud interpreted as expressing her wish to see a man she admired who would attend the nephew's funeral (*The Interpretation of Dreams*, SE 4:152–154); on the subject in general he says,

> Another group of dreams which may be described as typical are those containing the death of some loved relative—for instance, of a parent, of a brother or sister, or of a child. Two classes of such dreams must at once be distinguished: those in which the dreamer is unaffected by grief, so that on awakening he is astonished at his lack of feeling, and those in which the dreamer feels deeply pained by the death and may even weep bitterly in his sleep.
>
> We need not consider the dreams of the first of these classes, for they have no claim to be regarded as "typical." If we analyse them, we find that they have some meaning other than their apparent one, and that they are intended to conceal some other wish. . . . It will be noticed that the affect felt in the dream belongs to its latent and not to its manifest content, and that the dream's *affective* content has remained untouched by the distortion which has overtaken its *ideational* content.
>
> Very different are the dreams of the other class—those in which the dreamer imagines the death of a loved relative and is at the same time painfully affected. The meaning of such dreams, as their content indicates, is a wish that the person in question may die (*The Interpretation of Dreams*, SE 4:248–249).

Note that at the end of Dora's dream, she "calmly" ignores her father's burial.

32. "She may well have sought in Mrs. K., whom Freud recognized primarily as an object of Dora's ambivalent homosexual love, that *mentor* who helps the young to overcome unusable identifications with the parent of the same sex: Dora read books with Mrs. K., and took care of her children" (Erikson, *Insight and Responsibility* [New York: W. W. Norton & Co., 1964], p. 173).

33. Marcus characterizes the postscript as a whole as "a group of added remarks, whose effect is to introduce still further considerations, and the work is brought to its proper end by opening up new and indeterminate avenues of exploration; it closes by giving

us a glimpse of unexplored mental vistas in whose light presumably the entire case that has gone before would be transfigured yet again" ("Freud and Dora," p. 263).

Chapter Four. The Meaning of Dora's Dream

1. Compare Gross: in certain dreams "the reference to time in the manifest dream is presented by a situation in which the dreamer suffers a frustration through time like the frustration of missing (trains) or waiting (for the performance to end). Those frustrations in time in the manifest dream are the distorted expression of frustrations in object relations *in the past*" ("Time in Dreams," p. 470).

2. Bruno Bettelheim's observation may be pertinent here: "Since ancient times the near-impenetrable forest in which we get lost has symbolized the dark, hidden, near-impenetrable world of our unconscious. If we have lost the framework which gave structure to our past life and now must find our own way to become ourselves, and have entered this wilderness with an as yet undeveloped personality, when we succeed in finding our way out we shall emerge with a much more highly developed humanity" (*The Uses of Enchantment* [New York: Alfred A. Knopf, Inc., 1976], p. 94). Bettelheim cites one of the most famous occurrences of this metaphor, the opening of Dante's *Divine Comedy*, in which another familiar feature appears, that of the guide.

Whether Dora is, precisely, "lost" in her "thick wood" is not as clear as it is in the fairy tales Bettelheim discusses, and she does not "emerge" from those woods in the usual symbolic sense. But the basic symbolism Bettelheim describes suits the motifs of the dream, especially in its context—the analysis—and a guide character, though refused by Dora, is ready at hand in the dream.

A reading of this archetypal sort does not preclude our reading the woods sexually, as Freud wants to do; in fact, the connections between self-knowledge and sexuality are stronger and more numerous in Dora's case than they might ordinarily be.

3. Could the whole strategy of defending Herr K. by attacking Dora have been Frau K.'s idea? When Herr K. first responded to Dora's father's demand for an explanation, he "replied in the first instance by protesting sentiments of the highest esteem for her [i.e., for Dora]. . . . A few weeks later, when her father spoke to him at B——, there was no longer any question of esteem" (*Dora*, p. 62). Perhaps when Frau K. volunteered information about Dora's reading habits she also suggested how that information might be put to use.

4. Elizabeth Janeway, "On 'Female Sexuality,'" in *Women and Analysis*, ed. Jean Strouse (New York: Grossman, 1974), p. 62.

5. This "return to her mother" seems to have been borne out by her later development: see "Dora's Loves" in the following chapter. On relations between Dora and her mother in the first dream see French, *Integration of Behavior*, pp. 14–22.

6. See Spanjaard, "Manifest Dream Content," p. 232: "One can view the dissociated stance of the dreamer's self in the dream as the equivalent of negation in waking life: the last bulwark of defense against that which must be warded off. In this situation, an empathetic evaluation is appropriate."

7. Dora did marry though not the young engineer; see Rogow, "A Further Footnote." In reporting on her later life, Deutsch writes: "At the time of her analytic treatment she had stated unequivocally: 'Men are all so detestable that I would rather not marry. This is my revenge.' Thus her marriage had served only to cover up her distaste of men" ("A Footnote," p. 166). In fact, however, Dora said no such thing; the lines Deutsch quotes are Freud's interpretation of Dora's refusal, in the middle scene, of the stranger's company—a symbolic refusal much more immediately connected with her termination of the analysis than with any intentions about marriage (*Dora*, pp. 119–120, 110n).

8. Calvin S. Hall has attempted to test the interpretation that "the male stranger of the dream . . . symbolizes the father": see his "Strangers in Dreams: An Empirical Confirmation of the Oedipus Complex," in *The Experimental Study of Freudian Theories*, ed. Hans

J. Eysenck and Glenn D. Wilson (New York: Methuen & Co., 1973), pp. 113–125. It would not be inconsistent with our interpretation to link Freud directly with Dora's father in the dream too; in either case (the stranger represents Freud; Dora's father represents Freud) Freud's status has changed drastically from what it was in Dora's first dream where he must be linked with Dora's father in his role there of guardian or savior.

9. "As a *woman*, Dora did not have a chance. A vital identity fragment in her young life was that of the *woman intellectual* which had been encouraged by her father's delight in her precocious intelligence, but discouraged by her brother's superior example as favored by the times. When Freud last saw her, she was absorbed in such evening education as was then accessible to a young woman of her class" (Erikson, *Insight and Responsibility*, pp. 172–173). Actually, Dora had begun these studies before her analysis with Freud (*Dora*, p. 23). Hannah S. Decker is more pointed on this subject: "A conventional girl of Dora's background was expected to marry and to run a household. Although Dora presented Freud with a great deal of evidence that this was precisely what she did not want to do, Freud was unable to respond empathetically to any of it. Five years earlier, in the case of Elisabeth von R., he had already indicated his uneasiness with girls who departed from the feminine ideal. . . . his lack of empathy with Dora—though entirely understandable [in that age]—further narrowed her already circumscribed situation. Freud interpreted elements in Dora's second dream as signifying her conviction that 'men are all so detestable that I would rather not marry. . . .' But he did not for a moment take her seriously. He assumed Dora would someday marry, and he patronizingly discounted her 'more or less serious studies'. . . . At the same time that Freud assumed Dora's eventual marriage and motherhood, he openly disparaged Dora's own mother" ("Freud and Dora: Constraints on Medical Progress," *Journal of Social History* 14 [1981]:454). Marcus also comments that "it is worth noting that Freud tells us nothing more about these" studies ("Freud and Dora," p. 251n).

10. Erikson writes: "The nature and severity of Dora's patholog-

ical reaction make her, of course, the classic hysteric of her day; but her motivation for falling ill, and her lack of motivation for getting well, today seem to call for developmental considerations which go beyond (although they include) the sexual conflicts then in the focus of Freud's studies.

"As pointed out, Freud's report indicates that Dora was concerned not only with the recognition but also with the joint acknowledgment of the historical truth . . ."; and, "To establish and share the historical truth may have been a need surpassing childish revenge; to call the older generation's infidelities by their name may have been a necessity before she might have been able to commit herself to her own kind of fidelity" (*Insight and Responsibility*, pp. 169, 174).

Mark Kanzer supports Erikson's reading: "Adolescent identity problems contributed a contemporary note to her repudiation of adult guidance. One cannot dismiss her decision to leave treatment as mere resistant acting out" ("The Motor Sphere of the Transference," *Psychoanalytic Quarterly* 35 [1966]:530).

11. "The question arises whether today we would consider the patient's active emphasis on the historical truth a mere matter of resistance to the inner truth; or whether we would discern in it also an adaptive pattern specific for her stage of life, challenged by her special conditions, and therefore subject to consideration in her treatment. For we may suspect that at each stage of life, what appears to us as 'acting out' may contain an adaptive if immature reaching out for the mutual verification by which the ego lives; and that, between adolescence and young adulthood, the pursuit of 'the truth' may be of acute relevance to the ego's adaptive strength" (Erikson, *Insight and Responsibility*, p. 170).

12. "In addition to its wish-fulfilling function [the dream] serves the efforts of the psyche in its striving for fuller living, better adaptation, and greater health" (Nathan Roth, "Manifest Dream Content and Acting Out," *Psychoanalytic Quarterly* 27 [1958]:553).

13. See Kanzer: "The disposition to communicate or to break off communications is manifested and most readily dealt with in the

transference neurosis, which is intermediate between dream and waking and provides the analyst with the opportunity to enter therapeutically into the dream" ("Communicative Function of the Dream," p. 262).

14. "The urge to communicate one's dreams was described by Ferenczi, who pointed out that the listener chosen for this purpose is preferably the actual subject of the dream. The urge to communicate, therefore, arising out of the dream may be seen as a continuation of a tendency within the dreamer to establish contact with reality, as represented by the day's residue" (Kanzer, "Communicative Function of the Dream," p. 260).

15. In later works Freud not only presents a more fully developed theory of the transference, but offers practical advice in handling it—advice which runs counter to his tactics in treating Dora. See "The Dynamics of the Transference" (1912), *SE* 12:97–108 and "Observations on Transference-Love" (1915), *SE* 12:157–171 as well as chapter 27 of *Introductory Lectures on Psychoanalysis* (1916–1917), *SE* 16. In "On Beginning the Treatment" (1913) Freud advises psychoanalysts to begin with a sympathetic attitude and to withhold interpretations until an effective transference has developed (*SE* 12:139–142).

16. "Was this necessarily 'an unmistakable act of vengeance on her part?' It can be taken with equal cogency as a realistic response to a therapist who failed to maintain a position of loyalty to his patient's best interests as she saw them at that particular time"; and "Dora's unplanned termination may have been 'an unmistakable act of vengeance' against Freud on a quite realistic basis in order to regain some measure of her self-esteem" (Benjamin Wolstein, *Transference: Its Meaning and Function in Psychoanalytic Therapy* [New York: Grune & Stratton, 1954], pp. 56, 57). See also Erik H. Erikson's comment on the same topic: "When at the end she left analyst and analysis 'in order to confront the adults around her with the secrets she knew,' Freud considered such aggressive truthfulness an act of revenge on them, and on him; and within the trend of his interpretations this partial interpretation, too, stands. Nevertheless, as

we can now see, there was more to this insistence on the historical truth than the denial of an inner truth, especially in an adolescent" (*Identity: Youth and Crisis* [New York: W. W. Norton & Co., 1968], pp. 250–251).

17. Marcus finds the entire passage suspicious: "Yet it [Dora's termination] could not have been so unexpected as all that, since as early as the first dream, Freud both understood and had communicated this understanding to Dora that she had already decided to give up the treatment. What is suggested by this logical hiatus is that although Dora had done with Freud, Freud had not done with Dora. And this supposition is supported by what immediately followed. As soon as Dora left him, Freud began writing up her case history—a proceeding that, as far as I have been able to ascertain, was not in point of immediacy a usual response for him" ("Freud and Dora," p. 259). In a footnote on the same page Marcus wonders what led Freud to hold such high hopes for success in the case.

18. But see Wolstein's reflection on Dora's motives: "The possibility that she was not in love with Herr K. might have been further considered. It might just as well have been the frustrations she encountered in a loveless relationship with her mother which were at the heart of the matter"; and again, "Perhaps Dora experienced Herr K.'s sexual advances to her as possible interferences in her relationship with Frau K. . . . she may actually have wanted to maintain some remnants of integrity in an inter-familial situation which certainly did not overflow with it" (*Transference*, pp. 54–55).

19. In a study titled, without any apparent intention of irony, *What Freud Really Said*, David Stafford-Clark improves Herr K.'s proposal significantly by putting Freud's suggestion of double divorce and remarriage in Herr K.'s mouth (New York: Schocken Books, 1966, p. 170). As Melvin A. Scharfman points out, there is little evidence to support Freud's supposition that Herr K. intended marriage ("Further Reflections on Dora," in *Freud and His Patients*, ed. Mark Kanzer and Jules Glenn [New York: Jason Aronson, 1978], p. 53).

20. Thus Jules Glenn declares, "She felt that she was being dis-

honorably seduced" and "Her pride and common sense were offended" ("Freud's Adolescent Patients: Katharina, Dora and the 'Homosexual Woman,'" in *Freud and His Patients*, ed. Mark Kanzer and Jules Glenn [New York: Jason Aronson, 1978], pp. 27, 28).

21. See Erikson's comment: "Dora, no doubt, was in love with Mr. K. whom Freud found to be quite a presentable man. But I wonder how many of us can follow without protest today Freud's assertion that a healthy young girl would, under such circumstances, have considered Mr. K.'s advances 'neither tactless nor offensive'" (*Insight and Responsibility*, p. 169). See also Marcus, "Freud and Dora," p. 254.

22. Philip Rieff comments on Freud's interpretation of Dora's reaction to this incident: "To charge that all aversions betray their opposite is as misleading as to accept all aversions at face value. . . . Dora could have turned down Herr K. for several good reasons. Perhaps, at fourteen, she had not yet quite the aplomb to relish an affair with the man who was, after all, the husband of her father's mistress" (*Freud: The Mind of the Moralist* [Chicago: University of Chicago Press, 1979], p. 81). Glenn, commenting on data collected by J. M. Tanner (*Growth at Adolescence* [Oxford: Blackwell, 1962]), concludes that "it would appear that in Katharina's and Dora's day preadolescence lasted longer than it does now; it started at the same age as now (or perhaps slightly later), but adolescence proper started about three years later. One must remember that the scene by the lake, which happened when Dora was sixteen, may well have occurred at about the time she had her first period" ("Freud's Adolescent Patients," p. 25).

23. Freud's conclusion that Dora's transference involved Herr K. (rather than her father) has been generally and uncritically accepted. Raymond E. Fancher's treatment of that subject is a good example of the difficulties this view entails if it is examined carefully. But Fancher also does a remarkable job of bungling the literal facts of the case history (*Psychoanalytic Psychology: The Development of Freud's Thought* [New York: W. W. Norton & Co., 1973], pp. 166–180). See the helpful article by Hyman Muslin and Merton Gill, who

discuss Dora's transference to Freud as well as the countertransference ("Transference in the Dora Case," *Journal of the American Psychoanalytic Association* 26 [1978]:311–328). Muslin and Gill support the plausibility of Dora's transference to Freud from her father, but do not exploit the theme of betrayal involved in that relationship and so cannot link Dora's transference with her motive for terminating the analysis. Neither do these authors devote much attention to the transference significance of the second dream. Other pertinent studies include Glenn, "Freud's Adolescent Patients"; R. Langs, "The Misalliance Dimension in Freud's Case Histories: I. The Case of Dora," *International Journal of Psychoanalytic Psychotherapy* 5 (1976):301–318; Karl Kay Lewin, "Dora Revisited," *Psychoanalytic Review* 60 (1973):519–532; Jean-Jacques Moscovitz, "D'un signe qui lui serait fait ou aspects de l'homosexualité dans 'Dora,'" *Revue française de psychanalyse* 37 (1973):359–372; Lacan, "Intervention on Transference."

24. "When the analyst's prejudices and presumptions (that is, his countertransference . . .) have misled him in his intervention, he pays the price for it on the spot by a negative transference. For this negative transference manifests itself with a force which is all the greater the further such an analysis has already set the subject going in an authentic recognition, and what usually results is the breaking off of the analysis.

"This is exactly what happened in Dora's case, because of Freud's relentless persistence in wanting to make her realize the hidden object of her desire in the person of Herr K., in whom the constituting presumptions of his countertransference lured him into seeing the promise of her happiness" (Jacques Lacan, "The Function of Language in Psychoanalysis," in *The Language of the Self*, trans. Anthony Wilden [Baltimore: The Johns Hopkins University Press, 1968], pp. 69–70).

25. See Erikson's evaluation: "She wanted her doctor to be 'truthful' in the therapeutic relation, that is, to keep faith with her on her terms rather than those of her father or seducer"; Erikson also contrasts Freud's clinical distance with Dora's likely need for a mentor:

"Young patients in particular appoint and invest the therapist with the role of mentor, although he may strenuously resist expressing clinically what he believes and stands for" (*Insight and Responsibility*, pp. 169–170, 173–174).

26. On the relationship between dreams and acting out, see Richard Sterba, "Dreams and Acting Out," *Psychoanalytic Quarterly* 15 (1946):175–179; Roth, "Manifest Dream Content and Acting Out"; Doryann Lebe, "The Dream in Acting Out Disturbances," in *The Dream in Clinical Practice*, ed. Joseph M. Natterson (New York: Jason Aronson, 1980), pp. 209–223; and Erikson's comments in *Insight and Responsibility*, pp. 170ff. and *Identity: Youth and Crisis*, pp. 250–252).

Lebe's generalization certainly applies here: "Action following dreams needs to be considered in the analysis of dreams, particularly in patients with acting out disturbances. . . . Their actions can be further associations to a dream, a continuation of a dream, or an attempt to resolve a dream.

"Actions by the analyst or therapist need to be considered as well. He can consciously, preconsciously, or unconsciously act because of a patient's dream" (p. 222).

Freud addressed the topic in "Remembering, Repeating and Working-Through," where he related it to the transference: "But if, as the analysis proceeds, the transference becomes hostile or unduly intense and therefore in need of repression, remembering at once gives way to acting out" and "The main instrument, however, for curbing the patient's compulsion to repeat and for turning it into a motive for remembering lies in the handling of the transference" (*SE* 12:151, 154).

27. Glenn elaborates on the difficulties: "She was still attempting to disentangle herself from her parental ties. Indeed, the fact that her father brought her to the analyst, as do the parents of many teenagers, is a reflection of her adolescent dependence on them. This common mode of entrance into treatment can create difficulties, as it did in Dora's case. The teenager's wish for autonomy leads to a struggle against the analyst, who is foisted on her and

who, in addition, is felt to be an agent of the parents from whom she is trying to break away" ("Freud's Adolescent Patients," p. 29). The second dream obviously presents a radical version of this attempt to break away.

This is not to say as some writers have, however, that Freud was at any point taken in by Dora's father, whose intentions he understood perfectly; see, for example, Michel Neyraut, *Le transfert: étude psychanalytique* (Paris: Presses Universitaires de France, 1974), p. 143.

28. "Dora herself was undoubtedly deceived in this relation [with Herr K.], but she did not resent any the less the fact that Freud was fooled along with her" (Lacan, "The Function of Language in Psychoanalysis," p. 70).

29. Glenn, "Freud's Adolescent Patients," p. 32.

30. This argument does not imply agreement with Hyman's opinion that "the trial and judgment of Dora" constitute "the case history's underlying imaginative structure" (*Tangled Bark*, p. 344). Rather, it is the trial and judgment of Freud's theories on dreams and hysteria which both structure and limit the analysis.

31. Thus Kurt O. Schlesinger, following Erikson's line of reasoning, writes that "Freud's emphasis on the endopsychic reality . . . and his concomitant de-emphasis of the historical reality . . . might merge, as far as Dora was concerned, with her father's expressed idea of bringing her to reason and dispelling the fantasy" (Untitled presentation, in "A Psychoanalytic View of the Family: A Study of Family Member Interactions," ed. John A. Lindon, *Psychoanalytic Forum* 3 [1969]:59).

32. Thus Erikson claims, "And, indeed, the girl had every reason to suspect the whole older generation of having conspired against her" (*Insight and Responsibility*, p. 169); Janeway writes, "Woman after woman betrayed her, the men she loved attempted to seduce her. Under the circumstances Dora's inner strength appears to me the most remarkable thing about her case" ("'Female Sexuality,'" p. 63). See also Marcus, "Freud and Dora," pp. 255–256.

Chapter Five. The Ideology of Sex

1. Freud, *Three Essays on the Theory of Sexuality*, SE 7:151 and "Female Sexuality," SE 21:226–227.

2. The case is important for feminist critiques of Freud not only because of the issues it raises, but because it is unique in the canon of his works. His other treatments of female sexuality can be classed as highly theoretical or as incomplete. In the former category belong *Three Essays on the Theory of Sexuality*, "Some Psychical Consequences of the Anatomical Distinction between the Sexes" (*SE* 19:241–260) and "Female Sexuality." The case histories in *Studies on Hysteria* (*SE* 2:21–182) date from an even earlier period of the development of Freud's theories, of course, and the patient most nearly analogous to Dora, "Katharina," was "treated" by Freud in a single afternoon's conversation while he was on vacation. The much later work "The Psychogenesis of a Case of Homosexuality in a Woman" (1920) offers some important connections with Dora's case but was, Freud makes clear, a very incomplete analysis (*SE* 18:145–172).

3. See, for example, the work of Luce Irigaray (*Spéculum de l'autre femme* [Paris: Les Éditions de Minuit, 1974]; *Ce sexe qui n'est pas un* [Paris: Les Éditions de Minuit, 1977]; Juliet Mitchell, *Psychoanalysis and Feminism* (New York: Pantheon Books, 1974); Maria Ramas, "Freud's Dora, Dora's Hysteria: The Negation of a Woman's Rebellion," *Feminist Studies* 6 (1980):472–510. Mitchell writes, "The first full case-histories after the *Studies in Hysteria*— Little Hans, Dora and the Rat Man—deciphered the operations of the Oedipus complex before it was fully formulated as a theory" (p. 62).

4. See also the dramatization of the case history by Hélène Cixous, "Portrait of Dora," trans. Sarah Burd, *Diacritics* 13, no. 1 (1983):2–32; Jane Gallop, *The Daughter's Seduction: Feminism and Psychoanalysis* (Ithaca: Cornell University Press, 1982), p. 132; Janeway, "'Female Sexuality,'" pp. 62–63.

5. Some writers have seen vulgarity in Freud's interpretations and hints of his revulsion at "perverse" forms of sexuality (Gallop, *Daughter's Seduction*, p. 138) or have suggested transferences or identifications involving Freud with Dora's mother or with Frau K. (Jerre Collins et al., "Questioning the Unconscious: The Dora Archive," *Diacritics* 13, no. 1 [1983]:41–42) or with the young governess (Gallop, *Daughter's Seduction*, p. 142). Several commentators have remarked on Dora's integrity and courage (e.g., Janeway, "'Female Sexuality,'" p. 63). Marcus achieves a balanced description of Freud's unexamined assumptions about female sexuality ("Freud and Dora," pp. 283–288).

6. Salvatore R. Maddi, "The Victimization of Dora," *Psychology Today* 8 (September 1974):100.

7. Erikson, *Insight and Responsibility*, pp. 166–174; *Identity: Youth and Crisis*, pp. 250–252.

8. Mitchell, *Psychoanalysis and Feminism*, p. 62.

9. Ibid., pp. 12, 128.

10. Maddi, "Victimization of Dora," p. 100. A more realistic assessment of Dora's opportunities—or the lack of them—can be found in Decker's "Freud and Dora: Constraints on Progress," pp. 453–454.

11. See, for example, the rather harrowing documentation in Ann Douglas Wood, "'The Fashionable Diseases': Women's Complaints and Their Treatment in Nineteenth-Century America," *Journal of Interdisciplinary History* 4 (1973):25–52. Perhaps the most thorough study of factors affecting Freud's attitudes—historical, sociological, professional, and personal—is Decker's "Freud and Dora: Constraints on Progress."

12. Marcus, "Freud and Dora," p. 287, n. 18.

13. Josef Breuer and Sigmund Freud, *Studies on Hysteria*, SE 2:131–133.

14. Freud, "The Psychogenesis of a Case of Homosexuality in a Woman," *SE* 18:164–165.

15. Freud comments briefly on Dora's mother only five times in the case history (*Dora*, pp. 20, 23, 26, 68–70, 75–76) and she is

mentioned briefly only a few more times than that. His chief report of her is his famous description of her "housewife's psychosis" (p. 20). Freud's main impression is confirmed by Deutsch ("A Footnote," pp. 165, 167) and by Rogow ("A Further Footnote," p. 343).

16. Decker, "Freud and Dora: Constraints on Progress," p. 458; Jerre Collins et al., "Questioning the Unconscious," p. 41.
17. Ramas, "Freud's Dora," pp. 478–485, 487–488.
18. Deutsch, "A Footnote," pp. 165, 167. Even at the time of the analysis there was at least occasional evidence of this identification; Freud refers to a period in which "for several days on end she identified herself with her mother by means of slight symptoms and peculiarities of manner, which gave her an opportunity for some really remarkable achievements in the direction of intolerable behaviour" (*Dora*, p. 75).
19. Deutsch, "A Footnote," p. 163.
20. Ramas, "Freud's Dora," p. 491; see also Lacan in "Intervention on Transference," in *Feminine Sexuality*, ed. Juliet Mitchell and Jacqueline Rose (New York: W. W. Norton & Co., 1982), p. 69 and Mitchell's "Introduction—I," pp. 11–12 in the same volume.
21. Ramas, "Freud's Dora," pp. 477, 478.
22. Ibid., pp. 487–488, 492–493.
23. Ibid., p. 492.
24. Lacan, "Intervention on Transference," pp. 67–68.
25. Erikson, *Insight and Responsibility*, p. 173.
26. It is rather difficult for us to tell how literally, and how erotically, we should understand Dora's "homosexual love" for Frau K., just as it is difficult to assess the exact nature of her feelings for Herr K. (as opposed to Freud's reconstruction of those feelings). In both instances there is good evidence to support some degree of interest and attachment, and there is excellent evidence for reading Dora's feelings for Frau K. as extremely powerful. What is missing, however, is a precision in terms and concepts that would distinguish more carefully among degrees and kinds in these involvements of Dora's, nor does the evidence survive in Freud's document

to allow us to make those distinctions in retrospect with much confidence. What is also missing is an effort to take account of Dora's age and the particularly adolescent nature of both her attachments and her difficulties: see, in addition to the Erikson passages cited, Glenn, "Freud's Adolescent Patients"; and Peter Blos, "The Epigenesis of the Adult Neurosis," *The Psychoanalytic Study of the Child* 27 (1972):106–135.

27. Much of this evidence turned up in the analysis of the preceding chapters; briefly, we should take note of the number and frequency of gifts Dora accepted from Herr K., of her friends' claim that she was "wild" about him, of her own admission that she "may have" once loved him, of the fact that she did not tell anyone before Freud of the kiss when she was fourteen, and perhaps of the appendicitis attack which Freud reads as a false pregnancy. See also *Dora*, p. 59.

28. Schlesinger, Untitled presentation, p. 58. See also Lacan, "Intervention on Transference," pp. 65–66.

29. Lacan, "Intervention on Transference," p. 65.

30. It was during an argument with him on this subject that she lost consciousness—one of the events which persuaded Dora's father to bring her to Freud for treatment. In her father's words, "She keeps pressing me to break off relations with Herr K. and more particularly with Frau K., whom she used positively to worship formerly. But that I cannot do. . . . But Dora, who inherits my obstinacy, cannot be moved from her hatred of the K.'s. She had her last attack after a conversation in which she had again pressed me to break with them" (*Dora*, p. 26). On this topic Freud says, "Her behaviour obviously went far beyond what would have been appropriate to filial concern. She felt and acted more like a jealous wife" (*Dora*, p. 56). Schlesinger accepts Freud's interpretation, calling "Dora's preoccupation with the theme of her father's affair with Mrs. K. . . . excessive and pathologic" (p. 57).

31. An insight into the way Dora's intimacy with Frau K. served both to recover some of her lost claim on her father, and to function as a necessary substitute for it, appears in Freud's remark: "An-

other time she told me, more in sorrow than in anger, that she was convinced the presents her father had brought her had been chosen by Frau K., for she recognized her taste. Another time, again, she pointed out that, evidently through the agency of Frau K., she had been given a present of some jewellery which was exactly like some that she had seen in Frau K.'s possession and had wished for aloud at the time" (*Dora*, pp. 61–62). See also Suzanne Gearhart, "The Scene of Psychoanalysis: The Unanswered Questions of Dora," *Diacritics* 9 (1979):125.

32. It is only fair to consider, too, that Dora may have had other motives for revealing Herr K.'s proposition. If she had been afraid of her own passion for him she might have tried to protect herself against future temptation by making the matter public. If, however, she was still motivated by a sense of outrage at his proposition she may have been attempting revenge on him. The question is whether either of these motives could have outweighed the value of the deep attachments upon which she had come to depend and which her action endangered.

Freud has no difficulty explaining Dora's action as long as he is arguing that her love for Herr K. is her most compelling motive (*Dora*, pp. 107–108). But in an earlier comment on Dora's action he had picked an entirely different (though related) motive—"I looked upon her having told her parents of the episode as an action which she had taken when she was already under the influence of a morbid craving for revenge" (*Dora*, p. 95)—and neither of these can be accommodated easily to his later emphasis on Dora's love for Frau K.

33. The connection between Frau K. and Dora's mother has been echoed, oddly enough, in slips of the pen by two different writers. Schlesinger writes of Dora that "her long-standing sexual feelings for Mr. K. were exposed. She had supplanted Mrs. K., who, in a striking parallel to Dora's own mother, was invalided and unresponsive whenever Mr. K. was around but blossomed out when she was with Dora's father" (Untitled presentation, p. 58). Ellenberger, who does not cite Schlesinger, repeats the mistake in his summary

of the case, "So we see how Dora's mother regularly becomes ill on the eve of her husband's return, whereas Dora is ailing as long as Mr. K. is away and recovers when he comes back" (*Discovery of the Unconscious*, p. 500). Both authors mean, of course, to draw the parallel between Dora and Frau K., who has momentarily been confused with Dora's mother.

34. Freud, as we have seen, argues that Herr K.'s intentions may have been "honorable" (if that is the appropriate term), but there is little objective reason to think so; Freud's judgment in this is very obviously influenced by the countertransference which blurs, for him, the sexist assumptions of the proposition.

Chapter 6. Implications

1. Freud acknowledged this limitation: "I cannot disguise from myself that the easiest way of making those processes [of dream construction] clear and of defending their trustworthiness against criticsm would be to take some particular dream as a sample, go through its interpretation (just as I have done with the dream of Irma's injection in my second chapter), and then collect the dream-thoughts which I have discovered and go on to reconstruct from them the process by which the dream was formed—in other words, to complete a dream analysis by a dream-synthesis. I have in fact carried out that task for my own instruction on several specimens; but I cannot reproduce them here, since I am forbidden to do so for reasons connected with the nature of the psychical material involved" (*The Interpretation of Dreams*, SE 4:310). As Erikson has shown in his seminal article, "Dream Specimen of Psychoanalysis," Freud restricted himself to a very limited interpretation of the Irma dream.

2. See Spanjaard who refers to this dream, along with the Irma dream, as examples of Freud's reliance on manifest content: "Employing the manifest dream content . . . he further discloses the infantile material as a background, but the interpretation of the su-

perficial and contemporary conflict is identical with the manifest dream content" ("Manifest Dream Content," p. 224). See also French who uses it to illustrate his theory of the cognitive structure of dreams (*Integration of Behavior*, pp. 11–25). French notes that "it is evident that this interpretation of Freud's involves not free displacement of energy along any available associative pathway but the substitution of one total situation for another" (p. 13). Actually, the relationships between the manifest content and the Freudian latent content even in this dream are more complex than Freud leads us to believe. A more complex analysis of Dora's first dream would lead to a reading different from Freud's in some important respects.

3. It should be apparent that Dora's two dreams, even separated by several weeks as they were, form a pair in some ways, a miniature sequence. Franz Alexander treated this subject long ago ("Dreams in Pairs," in *The Psychoanalytic Reader*, ed. Robert Fleiss [New York: International Universities Press, 1948], pp. 336–342). For good surveys of recent research on the thematic continuity and development of dreams in sequences see Richard M. Jones (*New Psychology of Dreaming*, pp. 46–50) and Dement (*Some Must Watch While Some Must Sleep*, pp. 62–66). Aesthetic readings of dreams in sequence would permit a much richer description of their continuity than has yet been attempted.

4. "Even if [the manifest dream] has an apparently sensible exterior, we know that this has only come about through dream-distortion and can have as little organic relation to the internal content of the dream as the façade of an Italian church has to its structure and plan" (*Introductory Lectures*, SE 15:181). By "internal" Freud means "latent," of course.

5. It would seem that Freud was seeing Dora daily, or that at least some of the sessions were only a day apart; in speaking of the first dream Freud remarks parenthetically that "Dora brought me an addendum to the dream on the very next day" (*Dora*, p. 73)—that is, the very next day after the second session spent on the dream (described in pp. 71–73); the last three sessions, spent on the second dream, were daily (*Dora*, p. 119). In "On Beginning the Treatment"

he writes: "I work with my patients every day except on Sundays and public holidays—that is, as a rule, six days a week. For slight cases or the continuation of a treatment which is already well advanced, three days a week will be enough" (*SE* 12:127).

6. The most thorough study of Freud's aesthetics is Jack J. Spector, *The Aesthetics of Freud: A Study in Psychoanalysis and Art* (New York: Praeger, 1973). On this aspect of Freud's influence Spector comments, "*The Interpretation of Dreams* contains Freud's two major contributions to psychology that have had the greatest impact on art and the criticism of art: his conception of the unconscious, and his theory of the pleasure principle" (p. 85). The artist Ben Shahn has noted with regard to nonobjective schools of art, "There has been no other time in history when just this art could have taken place. It had to be preceded by Freud; it must necessarily be directed toward a public conversant with Freud, and in many cases the very suppositions upon which contemporary art is based are derived from Freud" (*The Shape of Content* [Cambridge, Mass.: Harvard University Press, 1957], p. 61).

7. "The contributions of Freud's theory of neurosis to the theory of dreaming cannot be overestimated. A preponderance of the hypothetical constructs which compose the theory were derived by analogical inference from the pre-existent theory of symptom formation" (Richard M. Jones, *New Psychology of Dreaming*, pp. 18–19).

Bibliography

Alexander, Franz. "About Dreams with Unpleasant Content." *Psychiatric Quarterly* 4 (1930):447–452.

———. "Dreams in Pairs." In *The Pyschoanalytic Reader*, edited by Robert Fleiss, pp. 336–342. New York: International Universities Press, 1948.

———. *Fundamentals of Psychoanalysis*. New York: W. W. Norton & Co., 1963.

Altman, Leon L. *The Dream in Psychoanalysis*. New York: International Universities Press, 1975.

Babcock, Charlotte G. "Panel Report: The Manifest Content of the Dream." *Journal of the American Psychoanalytic Association* 14 (1966):154–171.

Bergmann, M. S. "The Intrapsychic and Communicative Aspects of the Dream." *International Journal of Psychoanalysis* 47 (1966): 356–363.

Bernstein, Isidor. "Integrative Summary: On the Re-Viewings of the Dora Case." In *Freud and His Patients*, edited by Mark Kanzer and Jules Glenn, pp. 83–91. New York: Jason Aronson, 1978.

Bettelheim, Bruno. *The Uses of Enchantment*. New York: Alfred A. Knopf, Inc., 1976.

Blos, Peter. "The Epigenesis of the Adult Neurosis." *The Psychoanalytic Study of the Child* 27 (1972):106–135.

Blum, H. P. "The Changing Use of Dreams in Psychoanalytic Practice: Dreams and Free Association." *International Journal of Psychoanalysis* 57 (1976):315–324.

Breznitz, Shlomo. "A Critical Note on Secondary Revision." *International Journal of Psychoanalysis* 52 (1971):407–412.

Chesler, Phyllis. "Patient and Patriarch: Women in the Psychotherapeutic Relationship." In *Female Psychology: The Emerging Self*, edited by Sue Cox, pp. 318–334. Chicago: Science Research Associates, 1976.

Cixous, Hélène. "Portrait of Dora." Translated by Sarah Burd. *Diacritics* 13, no. 1 (1983):2–32.

Collins, Jerre; Green, J. Ray; Lydon, Mary; Sachner, Mark; and Skoller, Eleanor Honig. "Questioning the Unconscious: The Dora Archive." *Diacritics* 13, no. 1 (1983): 37–42.

Curtis, H. C., and Sachs, D. M., reporters. "Dialogue on 'The Changing Use of Dreams in Psychoanalytic Practice.'" *International Journal of Psychoanalysis* 57 (1976):343–354.

Dadoun, Roger. *Freud*. Paris: Pierre Belfond, 1982.

Decker, Hannah S. "Freud and Dora: Constraints on Medical Progress." *Journal of Social History* 14 (1981):445–464.

———. "The Choice of a Name: 'Dora' and Freud's Relationship with Breuer." *Journal of the American Psychoanalytic Association* 30 (1982):113–136.

Dement, William C. *Some Must Watch While Some Must Sleep*. New York: W. W. Norton & Co., 1976.

Deutsch, Felix. "A Footnote to Freud's 'Fragment of an Analysis of a Case of Hysteria.'" *Psychoanalytic Quarterly* 26 (1957):159–167.

Edelson, Marshall. "Language and Dreams: *The Interpretation of Dreams* Revisited." *The Psychoanalytic Study of the Child* 27 (1972):203–282.

———. *Language and Interpretation in Psychoanalysis*. New Haven: Yale University Press, 1975.

Eissler, K. R. "A Note on Trauma, Dream Anxiety and Schizophrenia." *The Psychoanalytic Study of the Child* 21 (1966):17–50.

Ellenberger, Henri F. *The Discovery of the Unconscious*. New York: Basic Books, Inc., 1970.

Erikson, Erik H. "The Dream Specimen of Psychoanalysis." In *Psychoanalytic Psychiatry and Psychology*, edited by R. Knight and C. Friedman, pp. 131–170. New York: International Universities Press, 1954.

———. *Insight and Responsibility*. New York: W. W. Norton & Co., 1964.

———. *Identity: Youth and Crisis*. New York: W. W. Norton & Co., 1968.

Fancher, Raymond E. *Psychoanalytic Psychology: The Development of Freud's Thought*. New York: W. W. Norton & Co., 1973.

Ferenczi, Sandor. "To Whom Does One Relate One's Dreams?" In *Further Contributions to the Theory and Technique of Psychoanalysis*. London: The Hogarth Press, 1950.

Foulkes, David. *A Grammar of Dreams*. New York: Basic Books, Inc., 1978.

———. "A Cognitive-Psychological Model of REM Dream Production." *Sleep* 5 (1982):169–187.

Fraiberg, Louis. *Psychoanalysis and American Literary Criticsm*. Detroit: Wayne State University Press, 1960.

French, Thomas M. *The Integration of Behavior. II: The Integrative Process in Dreams*. Chicago: University of Chicago Press, 1954.

French, Thomas M., and Fromm, Erika. *Dream Interpretation: A New Approach*. New York: Basic Books, Inc., 1964.

Freud, Anna. *The Ego and the Mechanisms of Defense*. New York: International Universities Press, 1966.

Freud, Sigmund. *The Standard Edition of the Complete Psychological Works of Sigmund Freud*. Edited by James Strachey. 24 vols. London: The Hogarth Press, 1953–1974.

———. *The Origins of Psycho-Analysis. Letters to Wilhelm Fliess, Drafts and Notes: 1887–1902*. Edited by Marie Bonaparte, Anna Freud, Ernst Kris. Translated by Eric Mosbacher and James Strachey. New York: Basic Books, Inc., 1954.

Galdston, Iago. "Dream Morphology: Its Diagnostic and Prognostic Significance." *American Journal of Psychiatry* 109 (1952): 287–290.

Gallop, Jane. *The Daughter's Seduction: Feminism and Psychoanalysis.* Ithaca: Cornell University Press, 1982.

Geahchan, Dominique J. "Haine et identification négative dans l'hystérie." *Revue française de psychanalyse* 37 (1973):337–357.

Gearhart, Suzanne. "The Scene of Psychoanalysis: The Unanswered Questions of Dora." *Diacritics* 9 (1979):114–126.

Glenn, Jules. "Freud's Adolescent Patients: Katharina, Dora, and the 'Homosexual Woman.'" In *Freud and His Patients*, edited by Mark Kanzer and Jules Glenn, pp. 23–47. New York: Jason Aronson, 1978.

———. "Notes on Psychoanalytic Concepts and Style in Freud's Case Histories." In *Freud and His Patients*, edited by Mark Kanzer and Jules Glenn, pp. 3–19. New York: Jason Aronson, 1978.

Glover, Edward. *Freud or Jung.* London: George Allen & Unwin, Ltd., 1950.

Greenson, R. R. "The Exceptional Position of the Dream in Psycho-Analytic Practice." *Psychoanalytic Quarterly* 39 (1970):519–549.

Gross, Alfred. "A Sense of Time in Dreams." *Psychoanalytic Quarterly* 18 (1949):466–470.

Hall, Calvin S. "Diagnosing Personality by the Analysis of Dreams." *Journal of Abnormal and Social Psychology* 42 (1947):68–79.

———. *The Meaning of Dreams.* New York: McGraw Hill Book Co., 1966.

———. "Strangers in Dreams: An Empirical Confirmation of the Oedipus Complex." In *The Experimental Study of Freudian Theories*, edited by Hans J. Eysenck and Glenn D. Wilson, pp. 113–125. New York: Methuen & Co., 1973.

Hall, Calvin S., and Nordby, Vernon J. *The Individual and His Dreams.* New York: New American Library, 1972.

Hartmann, E. "Discussion of 'The Changing Use of Dreams in Psychoanalytic Practice': The Dream as the 'Royal Road' to the Biology of the Mental Apparatus." *International Journal of Psychoanalysis* 57 (1976):331–334.

Hartmann, Heinz. *Ego Psychology and the Problem of Adaptation.* New York: International Universities Press, 1939.

Hawkins, David R. "A Review of Psychoanalytic Dream Theory in the Light of Recent Psycho-physiological Studies of Sleep and Dreaming." *British Journal of Medical Psychology* 39 (1966):85–104.

Hertz, Neil. "Dora's Secrets, Freud's Techniques." *Diacritics* 13, no. 1 (1983):65–76.

Hillman, James. *The Dream and the Underworld*. New York: Harper and Row, 1979.

Hoffman, F. J. *Freudianism and the Literary Mind*. Baton Rouge: Louisiana State University Press, 1945.

Hollande, Claude. "A propos de l'identification hystérique." *Revue française de psychanalyse* 37 (1973):323–330.

Hyman, Stanley Edgar. *The Tangled Bark*. New York: Atheneum, 1962.

Irigaray, Luce. *Spéculum de l'autre femme*. Paris: Les Éditions de Minuit, 1974.

———. *Ce sexe qui n'est pas un*. Paris: Les Éditions de Minuit, 1977.

Jahoda, Marie. *Freud and the Dilemmas of Psychology*. New York: Basic Books, Inc., 1977.

Janeway, Elizabeth. "On 'Female Sexuality.'" In *Women and Analysis*, edited by Jean Strouse, pp. 57–70. New York: Grossman, 1974.

Jones, Ernest. *The Life and Work of Sigmund Freud*. 3 vols. New York: Basic Books, Inc., 1953–1957.

Jones, Richard M. *Ego Synthesis in Dreams*. Cambridge, Mass.: Schenkman Publishing Co., 1962.

———. *The New Psychology of Dreaming*. New York: Penguin Books, 1978.

Jung, Carl G. *Dreams*. Translated by R.F.C. Hull. Princeton: Princeton University Press, 1974.

Kanzer, Mark. "The Communicative Function of the Dream." *International Journal of Psychoanalysis* 36 (1955):260–266.

———. "The Motor Sphere of the Transference." *Psychoanalytic Quarterly* 35 (1966):522–539.

———. "Dora's Imagery: The Flight from a Burning House." In *Freud and His Patients*, edited by Mark Kanzer and Jules Glenn, pp. 72–82. New York: Jason Aronson, 1978.

Khan, M. Masud R. "The Changing Use of Dreams in Psychoanalytic Practice: In Search of the Dreaming Experience." *International Journal of Psychoanalysis* 57 (1976):325–330.

Klauber, John. "On the Significance of Reporting Dreams in Psycho-Analysis." *International Journal of Psychoanalysis* 48 (1967):424–432.

Kramer, Milton, ed. *Dream Psychology and the New Biology of Dreaming*. Springfield, Ill.: Charles C. Thomas, 1969.

Kris, Ernst. *Psychoanalytic Explorations in Art*. London: Allen & Unwin, Ltd., 1953.

Lacan, Jacques. "Intervention sur le transfert." In *Écrits*, pp. 215–226. Paris: Éditions de Seuil, 1966. Translated by Jacqueline Rose, under the title "Intervention on Transference." In *Feminine Sexuality*, edited by Juliet Mitchell and Jacqueline Rose, pp. 61–73. New York: W. W. Norton & Co., 1982.

———. "The Function of Language in Psychoanalysis." In *The Language of the Self*, translated by Anthony Wilden. Baltimore: The Johns Hopkins University Press, 1968.

Langs, R. "The Misalliance Dimension in Freud's Case Histories: I. The Case of Dora." *International Journal of Psychoanalytic Psychotherapy* 5 (1976):301–318.

Lebe, Doryann. "The Dream in Acting Out Disturbances." In *The Dream in Clinical Practice*, edited by Joseph M. Natterson, pp. 209–223. New York: Jason Aronson, 1980.

Lewin, Bertram D. "The Train Ride: A Study of One of Freud's Figures of Speech." *Psychoanalytic Quarterly* 39 (1970):71–89.

Lewin, Karl Kay. "Dora Revisited." *Psychoanalytic Review* 60 (1973):519–532.

Lubtchansky, Jacqueline. "Le point de vue économique dans l'hystérie a partir de la notion de traumatisme dans l'oeuvre de Freud." *Revue française de psychanalyse* 37 (1973):373–405.

Maddi, Salvatore R. "The Victimization of Dora." *Psychology Today* 8 (September 1974):91–100.

Major, Rene. "Introduction: Un non d'amour." *Revue française de psychanalyse* 37 (1973):299–302.

———. "L'hystérie: rêve et révolution." *Revue française de psychanalyse* 37 (1973):303–312.

Mannoni, Octave. "Fiction I: Viennoise." In *Fictions freudiennes*, pp. 11–22. Paris: Éditions du Seuil, 1978.

Marcus, Steven. "Freud and Dora: Story, History, Case History." In *Representations*, pp. 247–310. New York: Random House, 1975.

Marty, P.; Fain, M.; M'uzan, M. de; David, Ch. "Le cas Dora et le point de vue psychosomatique." *Revue française de psychanalyse* 32 (1968):679–714.

Masserman, Jules H., ed. *Dream Dynamics*. New York: Grune & Stratton, 1971.

Mattoon, Mary Ann. *Applied Dream Analysis: A Jungian Approach*. Washington, D.C.: V. H. Winston & Sons, 1978.

Miller, Milton L. "Ego Functioning in Two Types of Dreams." *Psychoanalytic Quarterly* 17 (1948):346–355.

Miller, Stuart C. "The Manifest Dream and the Appearance of Color in Dreams." *International Journal of Psychoanalysis* 45 (1964):512–518.

Mitchell, Juliet. *Psychoanalysis and Feminism*. New York: Pantheon Books, 1974.

Morrison, Claudia A. *Freud and the Critic: The Early Use of Depth Psychology in Literary Criticism*. Chapel Hill: University of North Carolina Press, 1968.

Moscovitz, Jean-Jacques. "D'un signe qui lui serait fait ou aspects de l'homo-sexualité dans 'Dora.'" *Revue française de psychanalyse* 37 (1973):359–372.

Muslin, Hyman, and Gill, Merton. "Transference in the Dora Case." *Journal of the American Psychoanalytic Association* 26 (1978): 311–328.

Natterson, Joseph M., ed. *The Dream in Clinical Practice*. New York: Jason Aronson, 1980.

Neyraut, Michel. "Le transfert de Dora." In *Le transfert: étude psychanalytique*, pp. 133–154. Paris: Presses Universitaires de France, 1974.

Noy, Pinchas. "About Art and Artistic Talent." *International Journal of Psychoanalysis* 53 (1972):243–249.

Paley, Marlene Gershman. "A Feminist's Look at Freud's Feminine Psychology." *American Journal of Psychoanalysis* 39 (1979):179–182.

Plata-Mújica, Carlos. "Discussion of 'The Changing Use of Dreams in Psychoanalytic Practice.'" *International Journal of Psychoanalysis* 57 (1976):335–341.

Prescott, F. C. "Poetry and Dreams." *Journal of Abnormal and Social Psychology* 7 (1912):17–46, 104–143.

Ramas, Maria. "Freud's Dora, Dora's Hysteria: The Negation of a Woman's Rebellion." *Feminist Studies* 6 (1980):472–510.

Rangell, L., reporter. "Panel Report: The Dream in the Practice of Psychoanalysis." *Journal of the American Psychoanalytic Association* 4 (1956):122–137.

Rieff, Philip. Introduction to *Dora: An Analysis of a Case of Hysteria*, by Sigmund Freud. New York: Collier Books, 1963.

———. *Freud: The Mind of the Moralist*. Chicago: University of Chicago Press, 1979.

Roazen, Paul. *Sigmund Freud*. Englewood Cliffs, N.J.: Prentice-Hall, 1973.

Rogers, Robert. "On the Metapsychology of Poetic Language: Modal Ambiguity." *International Journal of Psychoanalysis* 54 (1973):61–74.

Rogow, Arnold A. "A Further Footnote to Freud's 'Fragment of an Analysis of a Case of Hysteria.'" *Journal of the American Psychoanalytic Association* 26 (1978):331–356.

Róheim, Géza. *The Gates of the Dream*. New York: International Universities Press, 1973.

Roland, Alan. "The Context and Unique Function of Dreams in Psychoanalytic Therapy: Clinical Approach." *International Journal of Psychoanalysis* 52 (1971):431–439.

———. "Imagery and Symbolic Expression in Dreams and Art." *International Journal of Psychoanalysis* 53 (1972):531–539.

Roth, Nathan. "Manifest Dream Content and Acting Out." *Psychoanalytic Quarterly* 27 (1958):547–554.

Rycroft, Charles. *The Innocence of Dreams*. New York: Pantheon Books, 1979.

Sachs, Hanns. *Freud: Master and Friend*. Freeport, N.Y.: Books for Libraries Press, 1970.

Scharfman, Melvin A. "Further Reflections on Dora." In *Freud and His Patients*, edited by Mark Kanzer and Jules Glenn, pp. 48–57. New York: Jason Aronson, 1978.

Schimel, John L. "The Semantic and Aesthetic Analyses of Dreams." In *Dream Dynamics*, edited by Jules H. Masserman, pp. 8–19. New York: Grune & Stratton, 1971.

Schimmel, Ilana. "Rêve et transfert dans 'Dora.'" *Revue française de psychanalyse* 37 (1973):313–321.

Schlesinger, Kurt O. Untitled presentation. In "A Psychoanalytic View of the Family: A Study of Family Member Interactions," edited by John A. Lindon, pp. 53–63. *Psychoanalytic Forum* 3 (1969):11–65.

Schneider, Daniel E. "Time-Space and the Growth of the Sense of Reality: A Contribution to the Psychophysiology of the Dream." *Psychoanalytic Review* 35 (1948):229–252.

Seidenberg, Robert, and Papathomopoulos, Evangelos. "Daughters Who Tend Their Fathers: A Literary Survey." *The Psychoanalytic Study of Society* 2 (1961):135–160.

Shahn, Ben. *The Shape of Content*. Cambridge, Mass.: Harvard University Press, 1957.

Sharpe, Ella Freeman. *Dream Analysis*. London: The Hogarth Press, 1961.

Sherwood, M. *The Logic of Explanation in Psychoanalysis*. New York: Academic Press, 1969.

Sicherman, Barbara. "The Uses of Diagnosis: Doctors, Patients, and Neurasthenia." *Journal of the History of Medicine* 32 (1977):33–54.

Skura, Meredith Anne. *The Literary Use of the Psychoanalytic Process*. New Haven: Yale University Press, 1981.

Slipp, Samuel. "Interpersonal Factors in Hysteria: Freud's Seduction Theory and the Case of Dora." *Journal of the American Academy of Psychoanalysis* 5 (1977):359–376.

Spanjaard, Jacob. "The Manifest Dream Content and Its Significance for the Interpretation of Dreams." *International Journal of Psychoanalysis* 50 (1969):221–235.

Spector, Jack J. *The Aesthetics of Freud: A Study in Psychoanalysis and Art.* New York: Praeger, 1973.

Spiegel, Rose. "Freud and the Women in His World." *Journal of the American Academy of Psychoanalysis* 5 (1977):377–402.

Stafford-Clark, David. *What Freud Really Said.* New York: Schocken Books, 1966.

Sterba, Richard. "Dreams and Acting Out." *Psychoanalytic Quarterly* 15 (1946):175–179.

Stewart, Harold. "The Experiencing of the Dream and the Transference." *International Journal of Psychoanalysis* 54 (1973):345–347.

Sulloway, Frank J. *Freud: Biologist of the Mind.* New York: Basic Books, Inc., 1979.

Ville, Evelyne. "Analité et hystérie." *Revue française de psychanalyse* 37 (1973):331–336.

Waldhorn, H. F. "The Place of the Dream in Clinical Psychoanalysis." *Kris Study Group Monograph* 2 (1967):96–105.

Willis, Sharon. "A Symptomatic Narrative." *Diacritics* 13, no. 1 (1983):46–60.

Wollheim, Richard. *Sigmund Freud.* Cambridge: Cambridge University Press, 1971.

Wolstein, Benjamin. *Transference: Its Meaning and Function in Psychoanalytic Therapy.* New York: Grune & Stratton, 1954.

Wood, Ann Douglas. "'The Fashionable Diseases': Women's Complaints and Their Treatment in Nineteenth-Century America." *Journal of Interdisciplinary History* 4 (1973):25–52.

Zilboorg, Gregory. *Sigmund Freud: His Exploration of the Mind of Man.* New York: Charles Scribner's Sons, 1951.

Index

Altman, Leon, 2, 6

books, 32, 62–66, 68, 85–86

Collins, Jerre, 106

Decker, Hannah, 106
Deutsch, Felix, 107
Dora's father, 27, 36, 38, 41, 44–46, 70, 72–73, 79–81, 83, 84–85, 87, 94–95
Dora's first dream, 43–46, 54–55, 116, 124–125
Dora's mother, 27, 74, 81
Dora's second dream: cemetery, 26; fantasy of defloration in, 48, 52–53; knowledge in, 24–25, 30–33, 35–37, 82; man in the woods, 27, 37–38, 84–85, 95; monument, 26, 155 n.10; structure of, 27, 28, 29; text of, 20–21; time in, 23–25, 33–36, 82–87; the town in, 47, 48, 84; train station in, 26, 35, 51–53; travel in, 22–23, 25, 34–37
Dora's transference, 44–46, 70, 73, 87–97
dreams: aesthetic coherence of, 9–13, 29, 38–39, 71–72; dream-work, 12, 14; empirical research, 5–7; latent content of, 3–4, 13–14; manifest content of, 7–8, 125–130, 149 n.11; and neurotic symptoms, 6; secondary revision in, 61, 134–135, 144 n.13, 150 n.12, 158 n.21

Edelson, Marshall, 6
Erikson, Erik, 101, 109

"five minutes," 53–56
Fliess, Wilhelm, 17, 42
Foulkes, David, 3, 6
Frau K., 41, 64–67, 73–75, 80–81, 83, 90, 100, 106–117, 162 n.32, 164 n.3, 175 n.26, 176 n.31
Freud, Anna, 143 n.11
Freud, Sigmund: "Female Sexuality," 99; his countertransference, 91–98, 122–123, 168 n.17; *The Interpretation of Dreams*, 1, 17, 62, 119, 130, 134, 136, 139; *Leonardo Da Vinci and a Memory of His Childhood*, 122; *The Moses of Michelangelo*, 122; "The Psychogenesis of a Case of Homosexuality in a

Freud, Sigmund (*continued*)
"Woman," 104; *Three Essays on the Theory of Sexuality*, 18, 99
Freud, Sigmund and Breuer, Joseph: *Studies on Hysteria*, 18, 103–104

governesses, 42, 58–60, 65–66, 81, 92, 96, 116, 160 n.26

Hall, Calvin S., 6, 14, 145 n.18
Hartmann, Heinz, 143 n.11
Hawkins, David, 2
Herr K., 41–42, 45–46, 65, 71, 73, 78–79, 83–84, 90–94, 96–98, 108, 110–117, 123, 157 n.20, 168 n.18, 169 nn. 21–23, 177 n.32
Hillman, James, 6

jewel case, 43, 108, 154 n.5
Jones, Ernest, 1, 17, 19

keys, 42, 53, 54, 55

Lacan, Jacques, 109, 112
letters, 31, 49–51, 105–106, 129, 158 n.23

Maddi, Salvatore, 101, 102
Madonna, 47, 52, 57, 109
Mantegazza, Paolo, 42, 64–65, 68, 96, 129, 154 n.3
Marcus, Steven, 18–19, 44, 101, 103
Mitchell, Juliet, 101, 102

Ramas, Maria, 106, 108–110
revenge motif, 49, 50, 51, 69, 70, 72, 73, 74
Rieff, Philip, 19
Róheim, Géza, 6
Rycroft, Charles, 6

Schlesinger, Kurt, 110, 111, 113
Sulloway, Frank, 18, 19

trains, 26, 155 n.11, 163 n.1
"two" (hours/weeks), 47, 57, 58, 59, 60, 61, 85, 89

"walking," 63, 66, 67
woods, 51, 163 n.2

Zilboorg, Gregory, 2